Actors Take Action

Date Due

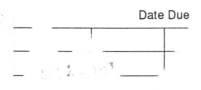

Actors Take Action

A Career Guide for the Competitive Actor

Brian O'Neil

Heinemann
Portsmouth, NH

Heinemann
A division of Reed Elsevier Inc.
361 Hanover Street
Portsmouth, NH 03801-3912

Offices and agents throughout the world

Library of Congress Cataloging-in-Publication Data
Brian O'Neil.
    Actors take action : a career guide for the competitive actor /
Brian O'Neil.
        p.   cm.
    Includes bibliographical references.
    ISBN 0-435-07012-6
    1. Acting—Vocational guidance.   I. Title.
PN2055.O55   1996
792'.028'023—dc20   96-14546
                                                                            CIP

Editor: Lisa Barnett
Production Editor: Renée M. Nicholls
Cover Designer: Linda Knowles
Manufacturing Coordinator: Elizabeth Valway

Printed in the United States of America on acid-free paper

99 98 97 96 DA 1 2 3 4 5 6

For Mary Dailey Frye
with love

Contents

Acknowledgments

I am indebted and grateful to the many people who helped to make this book a reality. Thank you Anthony Gentile Jr., Anthony Gentile Sr., John Gentile, Jenny Gentile, Donna Daley, Robert Rigley, Brick Karnes, Stephen Gregory, Joseph Savant, Michael Damian, Marc Kudisch, Ida Zecco, Steve Carson, Jeffrey J. Gill, Tony Nicosia, Holly Lebed, Paul Anthony Stewart, Mimi Hines, Robert Todd, Fr. Steven Harris, Gabrielle Winkel, and Nancy Barry.

Special thanks to my editor, Lisa A. Barnett, and her associates Cheryl Kimball, Heather Smith, and Renée Nicholls for their ongoing support. For all that I learned in our association together, I am always grateful to Meg Ryan, Matthew Broderick, and Fifi Oscard. Many thanks to my agent, Barbara Hogenson, and to Andrea Frierson, Paul dePasquale, Rosemary Keough, David Cleaver, Carl Afarian, Stan Yukinaga, Domenic Silipo, Josh Rivera, Beth Cash, Christina deLancie, Michael Howard, Michael Harney, Ron Stetson, and JoAnna Beckson. And, of course, thanks to Mom, Kerry, Chris, Marie, Michael, Cheryl, Joe, and Liz O'Neil.

Last, but not least, my thanks to the many actors with whom I meet and work. *Sine qua non.* You are the book.

Introduction

> Amateurs hope. Professionals work.
> —*Garson Kanin*

When *Acting As a Business: Strategies for Success* was published in 1993, no one was more surprised (or delighted) by the reaction it drew from the acting community than I. About three days after it hit the bookstores, I was asked, "Are you going to write another one?" Flattered though I was, I felt—I can only suppose—like the mother who has just given birth and is surrounded by well-meaning relatives inquiring about "the next one." In any case, I didn't give the question much thought for one simple reason: *What would it be about?*

Acting As a Business had found its form and content in the simplest way. It was based on the one-on-one career-planning sessions I had conducted with actors on a daily basis over a period of several years, as well as on my own experiences as a former actor, talent agent, and personal manager. The career-planning sessions, in turn, had found their form and content from the questions actors had asked me each day. A pattern had evolved because actors almost always asked the very same questions! "How do I follow up on an interview with an agent?" Or, "How do I get a good audition *without* an agent?" And the like. Almost always the answers could be found in a single word—the one that appears on a sign in the office of the co-founder of Creative Artists Agency and now Walt Disney Co. president, Michael Ovitz—*communicate.*

The success rate reported by actors who have implemented the suggestions and strategies outlined in *Acting As a Business* has been remarkably high. And so it continues that actors ask me questions. Different questions from those in *Acting As a Business,* but nonetheless, the *same* different questions!

Hence, a sequel. As such, *Actors Take Action* is meant to be read in conjunction with *Acting As a Business.* New issues are explored here, and some old ones—most notably, getting and working with agents—are reexamined and elaborated upon in far greater detail. Like *Acting As a Business,* this book moves in sequence from a discussion of issues facing the newcomer to topics that concern the more advanced and seasoned professional. References to *Acting As a Business (AAB)* contain the page numbers specific to the discussion at hand. While *Actors Take Action* offers no rah-rah formula guaranteeing stardom to its reader, the ideas expressed herein are, like those of its predecessor, both practical and proven.

More than ever before, actors are part of a corporate, global, and *competitive* entertainment industry—remember just a few years ago when we called it *show business?* Alas, the term has almost become obsolete. I have written this book, then, to give the actor more specific guidelines for creating career-advancing opportunities, as well as further instruction in the art of effective business communication. More information, then, is provided to help the actor *compete.*

For best results, please read *Actors Take Action* in its entirety before implementing any of the procedures outlined. If there are topics you would like to see discussed in future editions, please drop me a line. I'd really like to hear from you.

Brian O'Neil
250 W. 57th St., Suite 1517
New York, NY 10107

Part One:
Getting an Agent

I recently graduated from college with a degree in theater and have just had my first professional photos taken. I am now studying acting in New York and am about to do a mailing of photos and resumes to agents. Should I focus on specific ones? Or do I mail to everyone? It seems overwhelming.

First, you should be aware that there are agencies that specialize in representing young actors. These agencies are often referred to as "kid" agencies, and I've seen many young actors overlook them—thinking that the agencies are not appropriate for them, or, perhaps, that they lack clout. Yet a really good "kid" agency has a lot of clout by virtue of the fact that it specializes in launching young careers. These agencies can be found in the talent agency section of *Ross Reports Television* (see Appendix D); their listings say such things as "represents children, teenagers, and young adults."

Depending on the agency, "young adults" often includes actors up to twenty-five years of age. Also, a "kid" agency has very flexible crossover potential for an actor to work in all areas—that is, with the theatrical agents as well as the commercial agents. Larger, "adult" agencies are usually far more departmentalized, and therefore this flexibility is often limited.

None of this is to say that you shouldn't send to the "adult" agencies as well, however. To make all this manageable, start by mailing your photo with resume attached and a cover letter to a *specific* agent at each "kid" agency (see *AAB*, p. 40 for a sample cover letter). Send your smiling "commercial" photo to *one* commercial agent, and your nonsmiling "legit" shot to *one* theatrical (or "legit" agent) (see *AAB*, p. 12). These agents are usually so categorized in *Ross Reports*. Since there are many more "adult" agencies than "kid" agencies, send your mailings to them in the same fashion as you send to the "kid" agencies—only do so in groups of twenty or

twenty-five each week over a period of several weeks. Stagger-
ing the timing of your mailings may increase your chances of
getting more interviews. Otherwise, you may hit everyone at
once during what may turn out to be—for agents—an inop-
portune time for interviewing. If you start to get responses
right away, however, immediately get the rest of the mailings
out so that you will be able to examine all your options where
representation is concerned.

For a more cost-effective way of doing all this, you can
simply drop off your photo, resume, and cover letter in an
envelope with a specific agent's name on it at the office of
each agency. Although larger agencies often have reception
areas for you to enter, smaller agencies usually have locked
doors and a sign requesting that you leave your photo and
resume in the mail slot. Whatever their policy, it won't cost
you any postage fees and you'll know it got there.

**I am in my early twenties and am preparing for
interviews with agents who specialize in representing young actors. I've selected contemporary
monologues—both comedic and dramatic—from
roles in which I believe I would be well cast. I'm also
prepared to answer the questions agents most commonly ask in an interview [*AAB*, pp. 50–59]. Is there
anything else I can do to prepare for these meetings?**

Yes. Whether or not you have any great desire to do television
commercials, it would be wise for you to learn how to deliver
on-camera television commercial copy. The bulk of the
income at most "young actors" or "kid" agencies comes from
commissions earned from television commercial residuals.
Therefore, it is a very common practice at these agencies to
test young actors' commercial potential by giving them sample copy to read. Very often, when actors arrive for an interview, the receptionist will hand them a piece of copy to "look

over while you're waiting." When you encounter this situation, ask if you can either step out into the hall for a few minutes or if you can use the restroom. That is, go someplace and practice it *out loud*. Many young actors who are otherwise well trained are unprepared for the "commercial read." And while agents are not always inclined to admit it, very strong judgments are often made about young actors' overall potential based on their ability to handle this copy. An actor's potential to work with a "young actors" agency, then, can rise or fall on this very issue. That is, if you blow the copy read, it's possible that you may never get to do those monologues. Therefore, you also may want to investigate a good commercial class or perhaps take a few private on-camera sessions with someone who specializes in this area. Either way, be sure to ask around, get opinions, and do some price-comparison shopping before making your decision.

Recently I attended a business seminar for actors. The instructor told us that enclosing a cover letter when sending a photo and resume to an agent is unnecessary because it's self-explanatory that the actor is looking for representation. My question, then, is this—do you really think it's necessary to enclose a cover letter?

I think it's absolutely necessary—for a couple of reasons. First, it's highly unprofessional (not to mention lazy) not to do so. Second, a cover letter allows you to *extend* your resume and even to put a current, or recent, time frame around the events of your professional life (*AAB,* pp. 40–41). For example, in a cover letter, you can say something like the following: "In the past month, I have appeared as Cathy, a day player role on *All My Children;* have been called back for Soho Rep's production of *Hard Work;* and have been accepted into Michael Howard's scene study class." Even though your credits and training will be on your resume, this presentation lets an agent know that your accomplishments are *recent*.

In other words, a cover letter can add a wallop to your resume. Your letter needn't be long or elaborate. A few brief sentences is usually sufficient. Also, I know of no agent—or other industry professional—who would even think of sending a client's photo to another industry professional without a brief letter enclosed. So, if *they* have to, *you* have to. And given that a cover letter allows you to elaborate on your professional status, you should *want* to include one. (By the way, I hope that seminar you attended was free!)

What is considered proper etiquette in addressing an agent in your correspondence? Is it "Dear Mr." and "Dear Ms.," or "Dear Ann" and "Dear Tom"?

Although our business is generally a rather informal one, your best bet where correspondence is concerned is to address industry personnel as "Dear Mr." or "Dear Ms."—at least until you have met them. While most people probably wouldn't take offense at being addressed by their first name, I have often known of eighteen- or twenty-year-old actors to write to older, distinguished agents or casting directors and address them as "Dear Bob" or "Dear Betty," which is both presumptuous and inappropriate. Whatever their age—or yours—you can *never* go wrong with "Dear Mr." or "Dear Ms."

I have heard pros and cons about the advantages and disadvantages of home answering machines vs. live answering services vs. voice mail etc. Is any one really *better* than the others?

No. It's just that people have personal *preferences*. What's important is that whatever you use has an area code that will neither incur a long distance charge to your callers nor—and this is very important—lead them to believe that you may be "geographically problematic." By that I mean that you could be perceived as not easily available for auditions, or, perhaps, not able to stay late for rehearsals. The latter is most important at nonpaying theater companies in major markets such as New York or Los Angeles.

Most working, established, and/or represented actors simply use their home answering machines—unless this would incur a long distance charge to the caller. But the great "live answering service vs. home machine vs. voice mail" debate makes perennial fodder for agent and casting director seminars. This leads to warnings such as "answering machines can break down" or "live answering services can lose your messages, or take down a wrong number, etc., etc., etc." Good grief, you can get run over by a truck for that matter! So get *something* that works, and be in touch with it frequently.

Oh well, here goes! Personally, I prefer "electronic" over "live" answering services. Then I know exactly the message I have left, leaving no room for human error—other than my own, that is. But as I said, this is a matter of personal preference. Actors' careers thrive with every and all manner of message retrieval systems.

Industry personnel seem to place a great deal of emphasis on an actor's training. Which category on the resume carries more weight—the training or the credits?

The credits—hands down. Although industry people sometimes contend otherwise, what actors have done and where they've done it arouses their interest more than where the actors have studied or with whom (Yale and Juilliard being two glaring exceptions). After all, industry-recommended resume format suggests that actors list their credits first and *then* work their way down to the training—not the other way around. In other words, order indicates priority.

It's only logical however, that when actors are just starting out and their credits are light, the training will make the strongest statement about the actors' commitment to their craft. Also, if actors have only obscure or minor credits, the acting institutions they attended or their teachers might be what is most familiar to the reader of the resume, and may therefore generate more discussion in an interview than the actual credits themselves.

Good training, however, is essential. I only wish more actors would take the benefits of the good training they've gotten and get their show on the road by creating more career opportunities for themselves.

I am about to do a mailing to a number of agents who represent actors for theater, film, and television. What is the best way to follow up if the response is less than I hope for? Do I call, write, or what?

Generally speaking, if you do a mailing to, say, forty agents, and two or three respond and have you in for an interview, you've done well. It's just the way the odds fall, and it's important to have a realistic view here. In any case, your best bet for follow-up will be by mail, *at least for starters*. Here's why. If you follow up by telephone to the agents who don't respond to your mailing—at least in major markets such as New York and Los Angeles—you are likely to be greeted by a receptionist whose response will be something along the lines of the following: "We look at the pictures and resumes, and if there's any interest, we'll contact you." (Listen to *that* forty times in a row, and then let me know how your ego's holding up.) Agents themselves also usually recommend a mail follow-up; it's painless for you, and it can definitely bring results.

This is where the postcard-sized photo of yourself comes in. In most cases, a smiling photo will be your best choice for a follow-up campaign, but if your nonsmiling "legit" shot is more becoming to you, then go with that—at least for follow-up to "legit" agents (see *AAB*, p. 12 for more on "commercial" vs. "legit" shots). Agents usually recommend that actors post-card them once a month with career progress reported on the back of the card, and I think that in most cases, this is the way to go. Don't feel the need to stick with just the postcard, however. Many computer-literate actors design note paper and cards or other such interesting missives with their image and messages on them.

In any case, if you have nothing new to say and a month has gone by, it is better to hold off until you have something to report. That is, it may be six or seven weeks before there is anything worth saying. So *progress* is as important a factor as the number of days that have gone by on the calendar. The point of the mail follow-up is to build credibility in hopes of piquing the agents' interest so that they will have you in for an interview or audition. What constitutes progress? Any roles you've gotten, obviously, whether it's theater, film, or television; staged readings; call-backs for *important* projects that you think the agent might be familiar with or that may involve prestigious individuals (directors, producers, writers, etc.).

Also, be sure to report any "direct requests" that you may have gotten. A "direct request" is when a casting director or director has contacted you directly—that is, without an agent—and asked you to audition for a specific project. Be sure to also send clips of any good reviews your most recent work has generated.

If this doesn't work, we move on to Phase Two. Calling them. *So when do you call?* The best time to call an agent (other than to be returning a call of theirs, of course!) will be after you have mailed them a flyer to invite them to see you perform. (For guidelines regarding agent/actor telephone protocol and etiquette, see pp. 25–28 of this book.) *Being seen in performance is singularly the most important factor in securing representation.* The point is this. If you've genuinely been building credibility and starting to arouse their interest by mail, the chances increase that they will (a) take your telephone call when it comes; (b) attend the performance you invite them to; or (c) ask you in for an interview or audition if they can't attend the performance itself but are still interested in meeting with you.

For a plan and strategy of attack geared toward getting quality theater auditions (beyond what the trade papers offer), see *Acting As a Business,* pp. 71–83. I'm not advising that you abandon the trade papers; I'm only strongly suggesting that you *add* to what's in them by creating your own audition opportunities. It's not only possible to do, but it will also give you a feeling of control—not an easy thing to have in the particular profession that you have chosen.

As an actor who works quite regularly of late, it has sometimes become necessary for me to turn down other acting jobs. In some cases, it's a matter of accepting a better job, or, at times, the gig is simply not financially feasible. Can I somehow report this work that I turn down—as progress of sorts—to industry people with whom I want to stay in touch?

Yes. However, you will want to avoid using the negative terminology "turned down" in your correspondence. Rather, say that you were "recently offered the role of . . . etc." "Turned down" immediately invites the question, "Why?" "Recently offered" has a more positive spin, and while it implies you've declined the role, this wording doesn't necessarily say whether you accepted the job or you didn't. If the recipients of this bit of news want to know what the upshot of this "recent offer" was, they can always ask you. But at the very least, they'll know that you *are* getting offers.

In *Acting As a Business,* you discussed the questions agents typically ask an actor: "Tell me something about yourself," "Which casting directors know your

work?" "How do you see yourself?" and "What have you been doing lately?" (pp. 50–59). Recently I've been meeting with agents, and there is another question that keeps arising. My friends say they encounter it a lot, too. The question is this: "How old are you?" It has been my understanding that as far as age is concerned, an actor is the age he or she looks. The actual fact of the matter is not important. If this is the case, why do agents so often ask your age? And what is the best way to handle this off-putting situation?

First, you should be aware that talent agencies are licensed as employment agencies, and as such it is illegal—technically speaking—for an agent to ask your age in an interview. Casting directors are employers, or prospective employers, and as such it is unlawful for them to ask your age, as well. However, when an agent or casting director asks your age, it would be unwise— obviously—for you to apprise them of the illegality of the question, which they are most likely aware of anyway. Therefore, here is what to do. Answer the question as if you had been asked, *"What age range do you see yourself playing?"*—which would have been a legally "acceptable" question on their part. Be sure that your answer is realistic by getting honest input from others, and answer in an approximate age span of five years, which is generally the age span that industry professionals will use to assess you. The younger the actor, usually the narrower the assessment of the age range. For example, very young actors are often assessed as playing ages sixteen to eighteen, or eighteen to twenty-two, or eighteen to twenty-three, etc., and older actors are often given wider age ranges such as fifty to sixty. You can also be nonspecific with the numbers and answer in this fashion: "I'm usually cast anywhere from mid- to late-twenties" or "I'm usually cast late-twenties to early-thirties" or even "I'm usually cast early- to mid-twenties, sometimes even younger—late-teens—when I work on stage."

Now, to answer your *other* question: If, for all practical purposes, you are the age you look, then why do agents ask you your actual age? Often, they are doing a figurative "short division" of sorts and dividing your age into your professional credits. In other words, for the age you are, have you accomplished much? Are you "moving," so to speak? This helps them decide whether or not you may be worth the required investment they must make in order to represent you. This is even more reason to duck the age question, especially if you look younger than you are and haven't done a lot professionally. (You should be aware that it *would* be acceptable for an agent or casting director to say to you, "Are you legally *eighteen* years of age?" But somehow I suspect that you're not especially concerned about being asked *that* one!)

When an agent asks the very common question "How do you see yourself?" [*AAB*, pp. 57–59], my greatest fear is that I will only be considered for a narrow range of roles unless I express a wide range of possibilities. It's my understanding, however, that to give them *too* broad a range is unwise, as it tends to confuse or overwhelm them. Is there a way, then, to state some degree of range without turning them off?

Yes, there is. However, you're right when you say that you don't want to give them *too* much—they tend to find it disconcerting. Yet there is a way to state some range and not risk losing the agents. The idea is to give them a *handle* on you— on where you best fit in, and, therefore, how to "move" you. In order to express range without being all over the place, your response should have a running theme, and you should try to *lean* in a specific direction. In doing so, you're not really obliterating anything else you can do; you're simply giving them a good grasp on you.

Say, for example, that you have a body of work that includes a good range of contemporary roles and some classical roles as well. Knowing that the majority of breakdowns that agents work on will be in the contemporary rather than the classical mode, you could start by saying something like this: "I see myself *essentially* playing contemporary roles, although I've done classical work as well." (You're *leaning* here, but you're not *excluding*.)

To continue your response, consider the following: What kinds of roles are you *most* often cast in? Where do you really shine? Think, then, about roles that are a combination of what you do *best*, roles that *also* blend with your own essence. So next you might say, "I tend to be cast as characters who are independent, strong willed, and down-to-earth. For example, one of my best roles was Martha Livingstone, the psychiatrist in *Agnes of God*. In a lighter vein, I've also played Heidi in *The Heidi Chronicles*. She's another self-reliant, strong, and intelligent character. Also, people have often compared me with Susan Sarandon, and I can see myself being cast in the *kinds of roles* she's often played—especially *as a character like* Louise in *Thelma and Louise*."

If you have a prototype who is a film star, as in the above case, fine. If you don't, I think it's unwise to force one. However, if you do have one, *link* your prototype to a specific role for purposes of clarity. Also, notice in the last example, where a film star is cited, that I have emphasized the words *kinds of roles* and *as a character like*. I'm suggesting that you do, too. Here's why: While most agents would encourage the kind of example I've illustrated, without this emphasis, some could misconstrue your answer to mean that you see yourself at a career level to be considered for such major film roles. When you're discussing plays, it's not a problem, as many actors will play the roles you cite. But for films, it's wise to clarify your point.

Okay, now let's go back and look at your answer. You'll see repetition of characteristics (stated slightly differently, of course), but you'll also see that the roles themselves are actually quite varied. You've stated versatility and range without being scattered and unfocused. So there is a running theme. The idea is to go for the *characteristics* and the *essence* of the roles, using similar adjectives, and then *slide* over using "leaning" terminology such as "on the lighter side" or "only with a more humorous bent," etc. Speak in *gradations* when you're sliding to different roles by using terminology such as "darker" or "even slightly quirkier," etc. This approach will ease you into talking about a role that is *different* from the previous role you've mentioned, but it still allows you to point out how they are similar.

Let's try one for a hypothetical male actor, who might say something like this: "The general profile of roles in which I'm cast seems to fit in a category of what I would call "outsiders"—ranging from very dark, edgy, even dangerous characters like Pale in *Burn This!*, which is a role that I've done, to the far less dark and more poetic "outsider" of Tom in *The Glass Menagerie*. In fact, directors and casting directors have remarked that I'm similar in sensibility to John Malkovich, who, of course, has played both these roles. On the more humorous side, but still dark and edgy and very quirky, would be a role *similar to the character* Christopher Walken played in the film *Biloxi Blues*."

Okay, are there similar characteristics here? Yes. Is there range? Yes. Is it confusing and all over the place? No. Note that I've mentioned *two* prototypes in the above presentation. Try to limit this approach to instances where there is a similarity in sensibility between the two prototypes—as would be the case with Malkovich and Walken.

Often when I'm working on this issue with an actor, I'll start by saying, "If I had two million dollars, and I was willing to produce a production on Broadway of any play you've ever done, and everyone in the entertainment industry would see your work, which play would you pick? And what role did you play? Why would you choose this play and this role? What is this character like?"

After we examine the first play the actor chooses, I might say, "Fine, let's try another. This time let's look at a comedy [or a drama]." It's fun to watch a pattern emerge.

As you think about these questions, remember that the roles you cite in preparation for the "How do you see yourself?" question don't necessarily have to be roles that you have *already* played; it's just a sensible option that you might use depending on the body of work that you've done.

Unfortunately, very few actors have an intelligent response prepared for this question. Yet actors who regularly work almost always do. Why? Well, because they have solid careers and are employed most of the time, it's not hard for them to cite the ways in which they tend to be cast. The point here is that *you're* trying to get into *their* league, and presenting yourself as well as they do creates a powerful perception of you.

For the most part, the usual response to this question that agents get from an aspiring or unestablished actor is a stunned look followed by a blank stare off to the left, while the actor's expression reads, "Hmm, I've never really thought about that. I wonder what that means. Let me see. . . ." Then the actor takes a long pause and fumbles for something intelligent to say. Let me stress that from an agent's point of view, this is not impressive.

Having once been an actor, I can understand and appreciate that you don't sit around all day thinking about "how you see yourself"; you are busy working on your work (although a part of that is, of course, to know yourself!). Agents, however, regularly pose this question as a marketing screen, and you need to have a thoughtful, intelligent response—one that is both clear *and* concise. In a recent discussion ten agents said that actors' lack of clarity about who they are and where they realistically fit in is singularly the biggest problem that they encounter in working with actors.

I know of a few agents who phrase this question slightly differently: "Name a role in a current production on or off Broadway, where you could replace the actor who is playing the role if he (or she) were to leave the show." Wow! You can consider this version of the query to be a combination of *two* questions: (1) "How do you see yourself?" and (2) "How abreast are you of what's going on in the business?" So do your homework. I find that "How do you see yourself?" is the question *most* dreaded by actors. Don't be afraid of it; *prepare* for it.

Note well: Everyone isn't going to see you the same way, so please don't risk paralyzing your activity by *over*analyzing this agent-oriented issue. Live theater allows you the greatest flexibility of range (age, physicality etc.). Therefore, *show up* for every audition that you think you're right for, give the best audition you can, and know that the "business" will guide you to where you belong, because in the final analysis, that's how it really works. *Trust it.*

The idea of asking agents who have seen my work if I can get back to them with specific projects seems like a good suggestion (*AAB*, pp. 67–69). But what is the best course of action if an agent should respond negatively to my request?

The best course of action is to keep looking for another agent! But I'm running close to 90 percent in positive responses to this one. I call this issue of asking agents if you can get back to them "closing the sale." The more an agent likes you, and the more you've qualified your request, the more likely it is that the agent will go along with you. When I say "qualified your request," I'm referring to the key words you might use. For example, you might put it this way: "*If* I hear about a *specific* project, and there is a role in it that I *really* feel I am suited for, or perhaps if it's being done by a casting director who knows and likes my work, may I give you a call about being submitted for that *specific* project?"

Thus stated, your proposition is riddled with qualifiers, which will help reassure the agent that you will be selective in your requests. The point is this. Regardless of the response you get, this method allows you to discover where you really stand with a particular agent. The worst that can possibly happen is that an agent might say something to you along the lines of the following: "Well, it's better to wait until you hear from me—it gets a little crazy here with phones, etc., etc." Okay, it's not what you wanted to hear, but *still* this is better than sailing out the door thinking you're going to hear from someone who in reality may not be all that interested in you.

Of course, this isn't to say that if an agent says no to your request to call that you'll never hear from that agent again. It's just a way to find out how accessible the agent may be, and whether or not he or she may be receptive to a phone call from you. Remember, like any good salesperson, "you've got them when you've got them," and you must make your request while their interest is prime. In order to make this request, however, an agent will have to have seen your work—whether on stage, in an office audition, or on your demo reel. Whatever the response, they'll have to respect you for asking.

Naturally, it's usually easier for an actor to tell if an agent *is* genuinely interested than if the agent *isn't* interested. Sometimes however, agents are vague, or perhaps just being polite. What are some clues that an agent you're meeting with probably isn't all that interested in you? That is, despite what he or she may actually be *saying*?

I would say that the clues range from the obvious to the somewhat more obscure. Some agents will be perfectly honest, and even painfully blunt, in telling you that they are not interested in working with you. Somewhat more obscure are comments such as "Let me know when you are in something," which is usually—*although not always*—a dismissal. *Sometimes* it is sincere. However, if agents are genuinely interested in the possibility of working with you, they will often ask you to bring in monologues or songs, invite you to perform a scene in the office with a partner of your choice, or else offer to look at videotape of film or television work that you may have done. The more marketable agents find you, the more likely they are to handle the situation in this manner. For one thing, they each know you are agent hunting, and if they don't offer you a chance to audition, someone else—who may find you equally marketable—probably will. Obviously, an agent who is genuinely interested in the possibility of working with you isn't likely to wait two or three or four months until you're in a production of god-knows-what and god-knows-where, by which time you'd probably be forgotten about anyway! Now it's *possible* that an interested agent will take that route, but more often than not, you'll be asked to audition.

Other signs of lack of interest? Requiring that you submit videotape of your work when the agent is aware that you have no film or television credits on your resume. Be wary too, of "Get new pictures, send me a couple when you do, and then we'll see what happens." (Or "Get new pictures, send me a couple when you do, and then I'll see what I can do for you.") Of course, there's always the old standby, "You're not in the unions, so there really isn't much I can do for you now." (This one is often a soft-soap catchall *excuse* for a genuine *reason*—that you haven't done enough professional work yet to be of interest to the agent.) Be especially suspicious of this one if they had your resume *prior* to the interview, in which case the agents already *knew* you weren't in any unions! Another common excuse for lack of genuine interest is the old "We really aren't taking on any new clients at this time." Typically this means, "We really aren't taking on any new clients at this time—until, of course, we see someone who just blows us away, and whom we think will make a lot of money for us. *That* person, we'll be taking on!"

I have a friend who is a casting director. I don't want to jeopardize our relationship by asking for professional favors, although I really believe he would help me if I asked. I'm presently looking for an agent, and I'm wondering: Is there a diplomatic way of asking for help without putting him on the spot?

Yes. Here is what to do. Tell the casting director that you are about to do a mailing of your photo and resume to agents. Ask him if he feels that there are any that you should be sure to include because they might be right for you—in terms of career level, type, or age range. This gives the casting director three options: (1) simply rattling off some names of agents (per your request); (2) giving you an endorsement by suggesting that in your cover letters to the agents you tell them that he *recommended* that you contact them (as in a referral); or (3) offering to call some agents on your behalf. In any case, your request will not put him on the spot because it doesn't force him to go to bat for you in any way if he isn't so inclined. People often like to be asked for help, and, believe it or not, it sometimes doesn't occur to them to provide it otherwise.

A short while ago I received my "eligible performer" card from Actors' Equity Association, which means I now qualify to audition for Equity productions (*AAB*, pp. 22–23). The word on the street is that these roles are usually precast through agents' submissions. What's the lowdown?

No matter how much gets said about this issue, actors so often continue to miss the point. I'm discussing it here—in the agent section—because the eligible performers' auditions (EPAs) have great potential to be instrumental in helping to lead the unrepresented actor toward representation. I'll get to that later. First things first. Technically speaking, it is not possible for an Equity production to be "precast through agents' submissions" because (1) by Equity regulation, auditions scheduled from agents' submissions must be held *after* the EPAs have been conducted; and (2) no contracts can be signed by actors until after the EPAs have been held.

Where EPAs are concerned, however, the actual job itself will be more realistically available in some cases than in others. For example, the venue in which a production is being mounted (Broadway, summer stock, dinner theater, etc.) is a factor that will often reflect the career levels of the performers who are hired. Yet auditions are about a far larger issue than whether or not a specific role is actually available to you. Auditions are a major way that casting directors learn who you are; discover what you can do; and, in many cases, are actually reminded of your very existence. Each audition, then, is a mini-showcase. If you keep this in mind, you'll probably find the whole process of auditioning at least somewhat more bearable.

To clarify what I believe is often the true value of the EPAs, let me liken the whole matter to another area of our industry. Nowhere is the pecking order of actors observed more than in the casting of major roles in major films; most major roles in most major films simply go to actors who are already playing major roles in major films! Obviously, actors penetrate this pecking order—but not usually as quickly as the media would like to have us believe. Studios and producers need to recover the millions of dollars a movie costs to make and promote before realizing a profit, and one way of enticing the public to the theater is to offer fare that features actors who are popular and have a proven track record.

Now, imagine that an unknown actor with virtually no professional credits manages to get—probably through an agent—an audition for a co-starring role opposite Brad Pitt or Tom Cruise or Julia Roberts. What chance would this unknown actor with no professional credits have of snaring said role? In most cases, virtually none.

Okay, now imagine yourself to be this actor. And an agent gets you this very audition. Would you say to yourself, "This *must* be precast. I'm not going to go!" *Of course you wouldn't.* The idea of getting this major role in this major motion picture initially may even seem realistic to you because an *agent* actually set up the audition appointment for you. What's more of a tease, you may even get a call-back!

But later, when you discover who actually landed the role, you will see that it probably went to someone who is already a name—or on the verge of becoming one due to his or her prior work. *Then* you might say to yourself, "Did I really have a chance? Was this *not* precast?" And in a sense, it probably was. They might not have known specifically who would actually be cast in the role, but it was most likely to go to someone in the category described above, or at least approaching it.

Now, your *next* question might be this: "If there were so many actors whom they would most likely have chosen ahead of me, why did the casting director grant me an audition in the first place?" The answer? This is what casting directors do. They meet promising actors. Something about your photo, your training, or something your agent said about you made the casting director agree to see you, even though he or she probably knew that you wouldn't be likely to get this major film role since you haven't done anything yet. *But,* congratulations, you have now entered the "pecking order"! You have begun the process of coming down the pike, as I like to call it, and practically everyone ahead of you went through it too.

So what does all of this have to do with the eligible performers' auditions vs. agents' submissions? Just this. Simply because an agent gets an actor an audition for an Equity production, especially a major one, doesn't mean that there is no pecking order being observed there. It is certainly nowhere near the degree that occurs with a major motion picture, but producers and directors of plays know and have hired certain actors before, and often will want to hire them again. This is the way of the industry; this is the way of the world. Frequently, of course, they too will hire stars—although not nearly as often as most actors have themselves convinced! So, simply because an agent is able to secure you an audition, you shouldn't assume that there may not be other actors who are already "ahead of you," so to speak.

This brings me to my next point: There are *reasons* why a lot of actors have been able to get an agent! In many cases, it is because these actors already have careers that they have built up *prior* to getting representation. In other words, they have often advanced *themselves* in the pecking order before piquing the interest of an agent. Nowhere is this more true than it is with careers in the theater, which—despite the way it sometimes seems—remains the most accessible arena of our industry. To repeat, besides having a shot at getting a job, which will be more realistic in some cases than in others, going to EPAs is a wonderful way for (here we go again) casting directors to (1) learn who you are; (2) discover what you can do; and (3) in many cases, actually be reminded of your very existence!

Consider this. If you get cast in a small production or a showcase and you invite all the major casting directors in town to come and see you, what can you realistically expect for a turnout? It's not that casting directors don't attend these events; it's just that they can't possibly cover everything to which they get invited, especially in addition to everything that they *must* see. Your eligibility card, however, allows *you* to go and present a brief showcase to *them*. And there is no other area of the industry where this is the case. Your eligible performers' card is something that you've earned, and you should take advantage of it. Think, then, of each EPA as a mini-showcase for *you*.

Let me finish by telling you a story. I recently met someone who has worked as an assistant to a major casting director for several years. He told me that many of the actors that he sees coming in through the agents' auditions now *are the same actors who were standing in line at the EPAs two and three years ago.* This casting director is now giving these actors appointments through agents because he knows and likes their work and is considering them for the roles being cast.

"How does he know and like their work?" I asked him.

"Often, it's through their past exposure at the EPAs," he said.

"And how often has this casting director been blown away by a great audition at the EPA and *not* given the actor a call-back?" I asked.

His answer was just as I suspected it would be. "A lot," he said. "Sometimes they're not right for the role, but that doesn't mean that he doesn't remember them!"

The moral of this story is that if you are auditioning— and you are auditioning well and often—it will come back to you in ways you may never even know. But it *will* come back to you. It's the way the business works. Also, remember that agents regularly ask actors, "Which casting directors know your work?" (*AAB*, pp. 53–56). Attending EPAs expands your contacts, and it strengthens your relationships with these casting directors. All told, I would say that any eligible performer who lacks representation is possibly sabotaging his or her chances of getting it by not going to EPAs. *So be smart and be there.* (Didn't know what a can of worms you were opening, there, did ya?)

I recently got my "eligible performer" card. I went to an EPA and did a monologue for a major casting director whom I was seeing for the first time. When I finished, she told me how much she liked what I had done, but told me I was not really right for the role. However, she said I was right for a part as a regular on a new upcoming prime-time television series that she was also casting, and that I should pick up my scene at her office on the following day. Although I

wasn't cast, I got called back and put on tape. I reported all of this to agents on postcards, and as a result, I not only got a couple of relationships started, I have also gotten in on more projects being cast by this same casting director.

Yours is not a question, but I'm including this here because it's a perfect illustration of the whole point. And not to diminish your achievements in any way—but just to let others know, this happens every day. It doesn't happen to *every* actor *every* day, but it does happen every day. Okay, case rests!

Here goes. I am an actor who has worked a lot, but not for a while. I don't have representation at the moment, and sometimes when I go to EPAs the casting directors will look at me and say, "What are *you* doing here?" because they know me from agents' submissions in the past. How does it look for me to come in like this now? And how should I reply when they say that?

First question first. It looks a heck of a lot better for you to come in "like this now" than not to come in at all, in which case they wouldn't be saying *anything* to you—and most likely not be thinking about you either! Next, when you are asked, "What are *you* doing here?" respond politely by saying, "I really wanted to audition for this production, and this was one way that I was certain that I could!"

Okay, here comes a little story. I recently worked with an actor who went to an EPA to audition for a casting director for whom she'd auditioned in the past through an agent. She was greeted with the "What are *you* doing here?" routine, just as you have been. She made light of the question and performed her audition, only to be called by this casting director at home a week later.

"You know," said the casting director, "I'd really forgotten how good you are. I have another role for which I'd like you to read."

Upshot? An important relationship was reestablished, renewed, and regenerated with a direct request from a casting director that the actor could then report as progress to other industry professionals.

Incidentally, in a case such as this, the direct request might be reported along the lines of the following: "As a result of my recent audition for Ann McCarthy for the role of _____ in the off-Broadway production of _____ , she has just directly requested me to audition for the role of _____ in the national tour of _____."

I have contacted a number of agents by mail over the past several months, and I've stayed in touch regularly with postcards reporting my career progress. I'm currently in rehearsal for a production that I think will be of high quality and will showcase me well. I know I should probably follow up with a telephone call after I send a flyer to these agents, but I confess that I really dread making these kinds of calls. Even worse to admit is that I'm not sure I even know what to say when I do. Agents can be really rude on the phone. That is, if you can even get them on the phone. And if they're not rude, they're usually pretty abrupt. So what is the best way to deal with this trauma? And why do I have it?

The reason you have this trauma is because you don't take kindly to being rejected or treated rudely or abruptly by someone whom you perceive to be in a very powerful position to help you get what you want more than anything else in the world. Sounds like a pretty human reaction to me! And don't let it disturb you that you don't know how to handle the phone call, either. I've had actors on hit television series who are in the process of looking for new agents, as well as actors from the graduate program at Yale, tell me the exact same thing. But before we talk about how to deal with the phone call, let's take a look at the "rude and abrupt" issue because it will help if you can see the whole picture.

You could, for example, telephone an agent and get two entirely different responses five minutes apart. I liken the situation somewhat to a restaurant. You could walk in when it's not busy and get attentive, courteous service, or you could come in a short while before or after and find yourself in a circus atmosphere. The only difference is that in a restaurant you're still more likely to get better treatment than at an agency because you have something the restaurant wants—money.

Talent agents, more than any other professionals that I know, live on the telephone. It is their lifeline. Sometimes they are juggling several calls at once, often from casting directors, and they absolutely must prioritize these calls. Agents (sellers) can't risk incurring the wrath of casting directors (buyers) by keeping them on hold, and therefore they must make fast judgment calls as to whom to speak to now and whom to call back later.

Imagine that right in the middle of this, an unsolicited call slips through from an actor who wants to ask the agent if he or she will come see a play the actor's in, or whether or not the agent has received the actor's picture and resume. The agent's stress factor heightens, and guess who gets less-than-cordial treatment? Not the casting directors! Therefore, unless the agent is doing nothing whatsoever at the time of your call, there's an excellent chance that your call will be an *interruption*. And, while it may not seem like it, it is indeed the *actor* who is ultimately being served in this situation since agents are in the business of finding work for their clients, and all of their actions are for the purpose of furthering that goal. You simply cannot take it personally.

If you have difficulty with that, you'll certainly find what I am about to say even harder to accept. Contrary to one of the most popular and persistent entertainment industry myths, an actor is *not* selling himself or herself. If anything is being sold, it is his or her *services as an actor,* which most "buyers" will not need at any given moment. I know that may seem easy for *me* to say, but I have found that actors who are able—consciously or not—to adopt this subtle distinction also are able to function better by realizing the assertiveness that is necessary to compete effectively. In other words, they work more often.

Okay, now that I've got you more eager than ever to head for the phone, let's talk about how to handle that call! Here is what you most likely will encounter after your sweaty fingers have pushed the appropriate buttons on the telephone: Your call is likely to be answered by the agency receptionist, or "guard dog." (I don't mean to be denigrating here. I'm referring to the *role* the receptionist must play, not the individual person.) As anyone who has been in this business for more than fifteen minutes knows, "guard dogs" are—officially or unofficially—usually in training to become agents themselves. The exchange might go something like this:

Guard Dog: Gotham Talent Agency.
Actor: This is Cheryl Lewis for James Adams.

At this point, one of two things is likely to happen. The receptionist may put you through to the agent's assistant ("Guard Dog 2"), or may continue to deal with you personally:

Guard Dog: May I ask what this is regarding?
Actor: Yes. I sent Mr. Adams a flyer for a production of
_____ at the _____ Theatre, and
I wanted to extend a more personal invitation to him to
be my guest at a performance.

One of a few things could happen here.

1. "Guard Dog 1" could now put you through to "Guard Dog 2," the agent's assistant, another person whose job it is to buffer and who is even closer to becoming an agent than "Guard Dog 1." (If this happens, you will then tell the agent's assistant exactly what you have told the receptionist.)

2. The receptionist may put you on hold and then return to tell you that Mr. Adams is "on another call" or "in a meeting." Remember that agents *really* are "on another call" or "in a meeting" more often than not, *and you will probably have to call again.*

3. The receptionist could return to tell you that Mr. Adams has your flyer and will attend if possible.

4. Surprise! Mr. Adams himself could get on the line. And yes, that does happen far more often than actors tend to believe. How do I know? Plain and simple. *I work with actors every day, and they tell me.*

Now, if Mr. Adams takes your call, tell him what you told the receptionist—that you have sent him a flyer for a production of _____ at the _____ Theatre, and you wanted to extend a more personal invitation to him to be your guest at a performance. And see what he says. As I mentioned earlier, even if he can't come, it may be that you have been arousing his interest with your progress reports, and you may be asked to come in for an interview or office audition. In any event, if he can't come and doesn't offer an interview, and you get a good review or two during the course of the run or have some other progress to report, be sure to send this information along with a reminder of the remaining dates of the performance to him as well as to all the agents with whom you have been communicating.

If all of this sounds more than manageable, let me make a suggestion. There are some very effective—as well as reasonably priced—publicists who actually enjoy doing this. You'll need to ask around among actors to find out who they are and to get a report on their reputation and track record. Publicists usually charge a flat rate, which the actors in the performance all chip in toward, and then *they* go after the agents and casting directors for you. However you decide to handle it, if this is a quality showcase for your talents and the overall caliber of the production is high, then you and your castmates should do whatever you can to get industry personnel to attend. Regardless of the results, you are likely to feel better for having made the effort, rather than later regretting that you never even tried.

I'm presently rehearsing for a production of a play that I believe will be an excellent showcase for me. The problem is that it's being done at a theater that's really off the beaten path—in other words, it's outside of the geographical boundaries to which agents are usually willing to travel. Realistically, I doubt that I can get any agents to attend. Should I try? And if not, are there any other measures I can take to maximize this opportunity?

I recently met with an actor who was involved in much the same situation. In fact, several company members of the play he was doing said that in all the productions that had been performed at this theater, no agent had *ever* made the required journey to attend! I told this actor that whether or not agents came to see him was not the whole issue and that he needed to look at the bigger picture. I reminded him that the play was a very good one, that the theater company had drawn up an especially attractive flyer, and that he should use this opportunity as a means for letting people know *who he was and what he was doing*. And so, despite the theater's location, he sent pictures, resumes, and flyers out to a number of agents and casting directors.

A week later, he called to let me know that as a result of the mailing, he had been called in by a casting director—one of the biggest in the industry—to read for the lead role in a production of another play that was about to be done at one of the most prestigious regional theater companies in the United States. The casting director said that although she was unable to attend the play, it was stylistically very much like the one they were casting, and if the actor was able to handle the role he was now doing, he could probably handle the role they were now casting.

The moral here is that if you're doing a good job in a good production, you need to let people know about both you and it. So, yes, in a situation like this—when you feel that actually getting industy people to attend is a long shot—there are still things you can do. For example, you can simply send out your photo, resume, and a flyer as publicity, and then *not* follow up with a phone call. In any case, be sure to highlight your name on the flyer with a bright marker. This approach is fine in a situation such as this; as we've seen, agents (and casting directors) can still call you in if you've aroused some interest. You will want to include a note, possibly a message jotted on the flyer itself, such as, "I know this is a bit of a trek, but if you can make it, you'll be a welcome guest. For complimentary tickets, please call me at _____ [insert your phone number or service]." Or, if you feel very strongly about the quality of your work and the overall quality of the production itself, you can write and let them know that you will provide transportation for them if they wish to come. And then you can follow up on this written invitation with a phone call. In any case, if you feel that this is a good production, at the very least let industry people know what you're doing—in whichever manner above you feel is most appropriate.

Now, let's talk about *another* issue: how to capitalize on this event to help move you into a more geographically viable showcase! In other words, you can use this opportunity to not only inform agents and major casting directors of your current activity, but also to inform or invite artistic directors and casting personnel of *other* theater companies that you would also like to work with. In other words, people in places that we might refer to as being on your "A list." What would qualify a theater company for your A list? Such factors as the overall quality and caliber of the work that gets done there; whether or not they get reviewed by the press; and, of course, geographical accessibility to industry personnel—as well as whether or not they attend productions there with any regularity. Of course, most of the above factors are part and parcel of the whole issue. The better the place you're appearing at, and the better the production you're appearing in, and the more industry personnel have heard or read about it, the easier it usually is to get them there. And if it's a really *great* production at a really *great* place, that's usually where they'll be going anyway.

Again, the procedure for starting this kind of campaign is outlined in *Acting As a Business* (pp. 79–84). In following this outline, you will have your own strategy and plan of attack geared toward the theaters at which you would like to work. You will be chipping away at "infiltrating" them, so to speak. And no one needs to know about it except *you* and them. *Telephone follow-up procedure here will be exactly the same as it is with agents when inviting them to see your work.*

The idea of all this, then, is to use your present opportunity to move toward a better one. In other words, think in terms of "marrying up." Sort of like the Kennedys did.

Several months ago, I dropped off photos and resumes along with a cover letter to a number of small theater companies. I have followed up with progress reports by mail (reviews, notes, postcards etc.), as well as by attending their productions (and, of course, letting them know I've attended them). Recently I performed in a production at a theater that wasn't on my A list. I telephoned those who cast

**at some of these A list theaters to invite them to see
me in this other production. Even though they
couldn't come, they were pleasant enough on the
phone, and several of them were familiar with me as
a result of my mail-in campaign. I feel as though I've
made a dent, and I'm wondering where to take it
from here.**

Your best bet is to keep doing exactly what you have already
been doing. That is, continue to stay in contact by mail, and,
by all means, continue to keep seeing *their* work. And also
continue to let them know that you have been seeing it! You
said that the people you've spoken with were "pleasant
enough" on the telephone. If you think that this might somehow be related to the fact that you attend their productions—
and they know it—you are probably correct. Not only is this
mail campaign of yours feeding them information that is
helping to build their interest in you, but also you are wisely
implementing another time-honored business principle: "I'm
supporting your venture; I hope you will therefore consider
supporting mine."

The next time you are appearing in a production—
whether it's in two months or six months—you should, once
again, try to get them to come. If they are again unable to
come—for whatever reason—I suggest that you make an
adjustment to what you said the last time you spoke with
them. This time, *conclude* your telephone conversation in one
of the following ways.

Say something along these lines: "I certainly realize how
busy you are. As you know, I would really love to work with
you [or "your theater company"]. So if you should be sched-
uling any general auditions in the near future, I would greatly
appreciate it if you would consider having me in."

An even *better* approach (but not always possible
depending on the nature of the productions they do—new

plays by unknown playwrights, classics, old plays by established playwrights, and so on—would be: "I certainly realize how busy you are. And I understand that you will be doing a production of _____ soon, and I would really appreciate the chance to read for the role of if it has not yet been cast."

Best of all, if possible, would be the following approach: Be specific (as in the previous case), but also give them a *reason why they might want to see you.* As in: "I certainly realize how busy you are. And I'm aware that you will soon be doing a production of _____ . If you haven't yet cast the role of _____, I would really appreciate the opportunity to read for it. I'm in the same age-range as the character, of course, and I [fill in here any comment that may pertain] (a) grew up in the Southwest and have a strong feel for this playwright's sensibilities, as well as the required accent for the production; (b) have performed the role before and have gotten very good notices, which I would like to send along to you; (c) have done several scenes from this play in class and have a strong feeling for this character and for sensibilities of this playwright; or (d) studied in London, and I'm very skilled in the exact British dialect required for the role."

I use these as possible examples *because I have seen them all work.* Those who hire take a shine to this approach. Some will be flattered simply because you are aware of what they are doing; it also tells them that you know what their needs are and why you believe you can fill those needs. Another basic sales technique for time immemorial, this is far more effective than the old "Hope you'll keep me in mind" approach, which not only borders on the preposterous, but also invites this unspoken question from them: "Keep you in mind for *what?*"

What do you see as the value—or lack of it—in the currently popular "paid" agent seminars? At these

seminars agents are paid (from the actor's admission fees) to lecture, and then each participating actor performs.

In general, the value of these seminars will be in direct proportion to the combined elements of talent, age, looks, personality, and career level of the participating actors as they complement the current needs, taste, career levels, and areas represented by the agent who is being paid to conduct the seminar. More specific, the results typically break down something like this. The greatest number of actors who benefit by such seminars do so in the area of representation for television commercials. Here's why. First, the demand to cast faces of "unknowns" will always be greater for principal work in commercials—which are brief in length and concerned mainly with "type"—than to cast principal roles in major stage, television, and film productions. That is, casting directors—and therefore agents—for television commercials will generally be less concerned with the career level, credentials, and background of an actor, than casting directors and agents of theatrical projects will be. In television commercials, it sometimes happens that the most important credit an actor needs in order to be granted an audition is a special skill—an athletic one, for example, such as playing tennis or golf. This is not to say that commercial agents go out of their way to find actors who haven't worked professionally, or that they don't represent actors already to whom they will usually give audition priority. It is simply to point out that an actor's credentials are not usually as important in the commercial world as they are in the theatrical world. "Theatrical" projects will usually require more substantial ability and, in most cases, weightier credentials on the part of the actor to be seriously considered for a given role. Furthermore, the ways in which the casting processes of these two areas are carried out are distinctly different in New York (although not in Los Angeles). Let's take a look at them.

When television commercials are slated to be produced by an advertiser in New York, the casting directors will, in almost all cases, contact *by telephone* only those agents with whom they wish to work. By telephone, the casting directors will tell the agents the specifics of what they are looking for in the way of actors. For a television commercial that is cast in New York, a prescreen of photos and resumes is rarely required. (This is not the case in Los Angeles, however, where a photo and resume prescreen *is* required by commercial casting directors. Unlike New York, commercial casting in Los Angeles is listed in *Breakdown Services*—the printed outline that agents subscribe to that gives the specifics of projects about to be cast.)

If a given New York agent gets the telephone call, he or she already has the confidence of the casting director. Therefore, many, or in some cases, all of the actors suggested by this agent will often be granted an audition. So, then, if a good New York agent sees and wants to work with an actor—regardless of age—who has a particular look, energy, personality, and/or ability suited for television commercials, the agent will probably be able to secure an audition for that actor when the agent is working on a commercial "breakdown" for which that actor is suited.

However, casting directors for theatrical projects, in both Los Angeles *and* New York, almost always require agents to submit photos and resumes of those actors the agent wishes to be considered for an audition for a given project. These photos and resumes are then screened by the casting director and, subsequently, audition appointments are scheduled. Since all agents who subscribe to *Breakdown Services* are free to submit photos and resumes of their clients for any and all projects listed, casting directors ultimately get hundreds—and sometimes thousands—of photos and resumes for each project. In most but not all cases, casting directors will be more likely to want to see actors with the most substantial credits for these theatrical projects. In many cases, of course, they will even be looking for name actors. Logically, the more substantial the credits, the more likely it is that the casting director already will be familiar with an actor's career. Assuming too, that the actor is right for the role, the better his or her chances become of being considered for it. If we also consider the time factor required in the theatrical audition process—that is, setting up of audition appointments, first readings, call-backs, as well as the deadlines casting directors are up against—we can safely assume that the overwhelming majority of actors submitted by agents for theatrical projects subsequently will not be granted an audition.

If we would agree, then—for the above reasons—that theatrical representation is generally more difficult to get than commercial representation—on both coasts—where lie the benefits in "paid" agent seminars for *theatrical* representation? And what breed of actor gets them? As with so many other things in life, the young and the beautiful probably fare best, especially if they have talent. The younger the actor, the less is expected in the way of credentials on the resume. After all, if they're just starting out, why would their credentials be substantial? The pecking order of actors is not so rigidly observed with the very young actor. This is especially true for projects such as soap operas, where the "look" will almost always be a primary consideration—one that usually takes priority over professional experience.

The next group to benefit in the area of theatrical representation will be actors who have attained something in the way of substantial credits—whether these credits are from Broadway, off Broadway, regional theater, or from film or television. While these actors may not be currently represented, their resumes might be strong enough for an agent to perceive them as "movable"—that is, able to compete with working actors who will also be submitted to casting directors for various projects.

This means that the older actor (which can mean anywhere from thirtyish and upward here) with *unsubstantial* credits will probably benefit the least in meeting agents for theatrical representation at such seminars. Generally speaking, the agent's feeling is likely to be that there are too many actors who are already known by the casting directors for this actor to realistically be able to compete in the casting process—*at least as it exists between agent and casting director.* Remember, we said that casting directors get hundreds of pictures and resumes from agents, and only a small percentage of actors are usually granted an audition. Therefore, the actor who has done very little professionally—and is no longer especially young—will most likely be considered a "hard sell" by most agents who represent actors for theater, film, and television. Please note: I am speaking about overall tendencies—not absolutes. *There will be exceptions.*

All of which means this. For the actor who does seek to meet agents and audition for them at seminars, I strongly suggest doing some homework prior to spending your money to meet with them. If you are a member of Screen Actors Guild (SAG) or Actors' Equity Association (AEA), go to the offices of these unions and check to see who else the agent you want to meet represents. How many actors' names do you recognize? What areas of the media do they work in? Can you get a sense of this agency's strengths? For example, some agencies have strong musical theater performers, others have several actors on daytime soaps, prime-time series, etc. If you are not a member of either of these unions, check the *Player's Guide* (in New York) at the Library for the Performing Arts at Lincoln Center. In Los Angeles, check *The Academy Players' Directory,* which can be found at The Academy of Motion Picture Arts and Sciences in Beverly Hills.

The New York actor should find out whether or not it is an agency's policy to work with free-lance talent or on a signed-only basis—as is the standard policy in Los Angeles. In some, but not all cases, this means that the agency only accepts actors who are already somewhat established (exceptions being made for the young and the beautiful, of course!).

In any event, if the agency works on a signed-only basis, it will mean that the number of actors with whom the agent can work will be fewer than if it is the agency's policy to free-lance. This is certainly not necessarily a bad thing by any means, but it does reduce your chances of being able to work with a given agent. It could also mean that as much as an agent you meet likes you, he or she may still need to bring you in to meet his or her associates—who might *also* have to approve you before a working relationship can begin.

All told, be a smart shopper. Some establishments that sponsor these programs have a set list of guest agents; others allow actors to pick the agents they want to meet by signing up only for the specific seminars that these agents are conducting. Also, some establishments require an audition for an actor to be part of their program; others allow in all who wish to participate.

Last, but oh-so-far from least, one vitally important question. Are you agent ready? Are your audition skills and personal presentation such that an agent might want to invest in your career at this time? Get input from your teachers on this one. If you're not ready, don't go!

None of the above is meant to be an endorsement or a denigration of "paid" agent seminars. It is only an analysis of observations I've made as to who benefits the most and why. Still, I believe the best way for agents to see your work is in a more viable venue, such as a play, even though it can be difficult to get them to come. Therefore, for the actor who participates in seminars or is contemplating doing so, here is a suggestion. Be sure to *also* put your time and energies into advancing your career, building your resume, and sharpening your skills in the more established and time-honored fashion. For a look at the benefits in attending seminars conducted by *casting directors*, please see Part Five, "Some Parting Pointers."

I have recently taken a series of seminars and short-term classes with a number of casting directors and agents. Since that time, I haven't had much success

**in getting hold of them by telephone to request audi-
tions for specific projects. It's made me more than a
little angry, as I considered this expenditure an
investment. Could I be doing something wrong?**

I'm not sure if "wrong" is the word I'd use here, but you'll
want to make an adjustment in your thinking. In other
words, you need to be clear about the difference between
what you actually paid for in taking these classes and what
you *think* you paid for. What you paid for was an evening,
weekend, or six-week class or workshop with an industry person who may have had valuable information for you. In other
words, you paid for a specific relationship, as in teacher-
student, for the duration of the specified period of time of the
event or the class. *Hopefully*, you learned a lot and got what
you paid for.

What you *think* you paid for is an *ongoing* relationship,
which is the hope one always has in taking such seminars and
classes, and is, of course, the lure of them in the first place.
You can't buy a relationship. Therefore, it will be in your best
interest to continue to stay in touch with the people you've
met—by mail—employing all the same progress-reporting
techniques that I have discussed previously. Remember, just
because the results you've gotten have been less than satisfactory so far, it doesn't mean that the situation will stay that
way forever.

**I am ready to do a big "push" for representation. In
the past, I've done some free-lancing and have
recently appeared on Broadway. Since the production has now closed, is there any way that I can still
make use of such a good recent credit?**

Let me say here that an actor who is currently, or recently
was, involved in a major production—be it a well-publicized
play, film, or television show—is in a stronger position to
make a follow-up telephone call to an agent after sending a

photo and resume than an actor who wasn't or isn't in the same situation. Many people are surprised to hear that actors such as yourself are not already well represented, and yet it's actually far more common than one might think.

In any case, here is what to do. One week after your mailing, call the agents you would like to meet but haven't heard from. After you give your name to the receptionist and ask for the agent with whom you would like to speak, the receptionist is likely to say, "What is this regarding?" Reply that you were recently in the Broadway production of _____ , that you sent your photo and resume to Ms. Smith last week, and that you were wondering if you might speak with her. I would not recommend handling it in the *reverse* manner of the above, such as, "I sent Ms. Smith my photo and resume last week, and I was recently in the Broadway production of _____ , and I was wondering if, etc." If you handle the call in this fashion, you risk getting cut off right after you say, "I sent Ms. Smith my photo and resume last week. . . ." The receptionist may quickly reply, "Well, if she's interested, she'll call you." In other words, always put your bait at the *beginning* of your conversation, not at the end, or you may not get to use it.

I am currently appearing in an off-Broadway production and am now looking for really solid representation. Do you have any specific suggestions I can implement to capitalize on my present situation?

Yes. Draw up a list of agencies that you think might be able to provide you with "really solid representation." Cull your ideas from what you have heard from others as well as from checking the agency client listings at Actors' Equity and the Screen Actors Guild (if you are a SAG member). Also check the *Players' Guide,* which you can review at Actors' Equity and at

the Lincoln Center Library for the Performing Arts. These listings will help you get a sense of the career levels and media
areas in which the clients of each agency regularly work.

Once you form your list, write a cover letter that begins
by telling each agent the name of the production you are in
as well as the role you play. Conclude—and this is important—by telling each agent that you would appreciate the
opportunity to meet with them at their earliest convenience.
Here is why: You are currently in a position to make an
investment in your career—and unlike performing in a
showcase-type production, where admission is free for agents,
you actually may need to *purchase* tickets for at least some of
these agents. By requesting a *meeting* first instead of making a
carte blanche offer of tickets in your letter—as actors often
do—you will be in a stronger position to discover if there is
any real rapport with a prospective agent. Otherwise, you
may be bombarded with agents simply calling you to score
free theater tickets—when their interest in *you* may not be all
that genuine. (Call me cautious, call me cynical, but yes, it
really does happen.)

Okay, suppose the response to your photo, resume, and
letter is less than satisfactory, and you want to do a phone
follow-up, which I *do* recommend in a case like yours. Start by
first calling the agents you believe you would *most* like to
meet. In other words, establish a pecking order. (After all, if
they can have one, *you* can have one!) In other words, if you
have initially selected fifteen agencies to contact, now break
your list down again to A, B, and C lists that each consist of
five agencies. Call the agents on your A list first, using a dia-
logue similar to that suggested in the preceding discussion,
and do your best to obtain some interviews. If the results are
not as spectacular as you might hope, then shift down to the
B list, etc. As I said, this campaign will incur an expenditure
on your part and will therefore involve risk, but if you are
judicious, it may also prove to be a business move that really

pays off. Even if your "interview" initially takes place only over the phone, this is still preferable to sending a written free offer of expensive theater tickets.

This very same procedure can be used by understudies or standbys who know in advance of those performances when they will be going on.

I recently shot a featured role on an upcoming episode of a television series. I got the job myself after writing to the casting director and then staying in touch with him. How can I use this to meet agents? Do I call them up and ask them to watch?

First, *write* to any agents whom you've met in the past and would like to stay in touch with, as well as to any *new* agents you would like to meet now. Tell them in your letter (or on a postcard if you already know them) the date, television station, and airtime of the show. If you have access to a computer, you can even make up a special flyer for this event.

If no one responds after the airdate, you can *then* call them. Introduce yourself and say, "Monday night I appeared in a featured role on an episode of _____ . I've sent my photo and resume in, and I'm wondering if I could drop off a tape of my performance for you [or for "Mr. Adams" if you don't get past the receptionist] to see."

Some years ago, actors who got jobs on television shows had to call up agents the day of the airing and remind them to please "tune in." 'Tis no longer necessary, thanks to modern technology.

By the way, I recently worked with an actor in the same situation as yourself. Because he appeared on an episode of a very popular series, he discovered when he made his calls that almost everyone on his list had already seen him on the show. "*You're* not represented?" they said. "Come on in!" And, yes, *that* really happens, too!

I live in Los Angeles, where there is a great deal of emphasis on having a video demo tape, or "reel." I am putting together a tape of work that I have done. Do you have any tips? Also, what is the best procedure for follow-up?

General consensus has it that you keep your tape limited to six minutes of your best work. Get editorial input on the order, balance, and pacing of the individual spots. Those who regularly view demo tapes—agents and casting directors, for example—usually develop a feel for the rhythm of a well-put-together tape, and the above-mentioned components greatly impact its overall effectiveness. Although the recommended order of scenes is feature film, made-for-television movies, prime-time television, and then daytime television (soap operas), this sequence can, and should be, precluded by featuring your best and most exciting work *first*. Also, many actors start their videotapes by presenting their headshot in the opening footage. This is a good idea because it shows the actor outside of a role, and it lets the viewer know immediately who will be the "star" of the tape.

Have your copies duplicated from the master onto VHS format cassettes. Many agents and casting directors end up taking tapes home with them, and most offices are also now equipped with this format. After your copies have been made, store your master tape at home.

In your cover letter, mention the names of a few of the films you've been in—or the television shows you've worked on—that are represented on your tape. Close your letter by saying, "I have a video demo tape of my work available for your viewing and would appreciate the opportunity to meet you at your convenience." If you don't hear from the agents you have contacted, call them to see if you can send or drop off a copy of your tape for them to look at.

As you know, it's very difficult for the Los Angeles actor to be considered for film and television projects without being signed to a good agent. The option to free-lance does not exist there as it does in New York, which makes a meeting between a Los Angeles actor and agent a do-or-die situation. Nor does the Los Angeles actor have the option of walking around town to drop off photos and resumes at agents' offices—and to cover a good portion of them in one afternoon. It's also usually harder to get L.A. agents to see a play you're appearing in. It probably won't be a dozen or so blocks from their office either—as it might be in New York. What does this add up to? Although New York is certainly tough, getting to meet and work with a *really* good agent in Los Angeles is—generally speaking, at least—even harder than it is in New York. Hence the need for especially assertive follow-up.

I have been in New York for a few years now. I've gotten good training, some stage work and a little film and television work, too. I have a good demo tape, and I want to check out Los Angeles. I have a few contacts out there who are going to set me up with some agent interviews. Do you have any specific advice for handling these meetings?

I'm assuming that you're not working with any agencies in New York. If you are, however, ask your agents here if they would arrange a meeting for you at their West Coast office—or with their West Coast affiliate if they don't have an office of their own in L.A. Often this gesture is only extended to an agency's *signed* clients, but if you have free-lance relationships that are good and solid, it's certainly worth a try.

Important. There is a question that agents will usually ask an actor who is just in from the opposite coast: "How long will you be here?" It's not fair for me to call it a trap question, because it really isn't. But what the agent is trying to discern, which will depend upon the projected length of your stay, is whether or not your career is worth an investment on their part at this point in time. Actors often make the mistake (and

I'll explain why I call it a mistake in just a minute) of saying, "I'm really just here to check out L.A., so I'm not sure" or "I'll be here for two weeks" or "I'll be here for a month." In *most* cases, the response to this will be, "Well, there's nothing I can do for you now, but be sure to get back in touch with me when you're here for good." Boom lowered! How often an actor will say to me, "But I *would* have stayed if I knew they were interested in working with me." An agent cannot be expected to put any steam into the career of an actor who's in town "checking it out" or "here for two weeks," etc. *Therefore,* if, and *only* if, you know that you *will* stay if an agent you meet expresses a strong interest in working with you, say, "I'm here permanently," or, at the very least, "I'm definitely here for at least six months" or "for all of pilot season and plan to relocate here permanently."

Again, *only* say this if, in fact, you will stay if they want to take you on as a client. I'm not asking you to lie. But if you don't follow this suggestion, you can probably expect virtually nothing in the way of a relationship, at least until such time as you move there. And by that time, they may well have lost interest in you.

I'm an actor living in Los Angeles who is thinking of moving to New York. I know that more actors do it the other way around, but it's what I want to do. Do you have any suggestions specific to this situation where agents are concerned?

Yep. This is an easy one. New York agents ask the same question I talked about in the previous situation. And for the same reason! Therefore, you answer in the same way (although it would be doubtful, of course, that you will be leaving Los Angeles to go to New York for "pilot season"!).

I am presently signed with a personal manager [see *AAB*, pp. 91–97]. My manager has relationships with

only a few agents, and activity is slow for me at this time. I've had some success with this manager, and I'm not looking to try to end the relationship, but I'd like to improve the situation where the agents are concerned. Is there anything you can suggest?

Yes. First things first. You say that "activity is slow" for you at this time. Does this mean that the agents are calling your manager to "clear" you for projects and then not succeeding in subsequently obtaining auditions for you? If this is the case, you need to ask your manager to find out from the agents *why* you are not getting the auditions.

If you mean that "activity is slow" because the agents are not submitting you for many projects, here are a few possible reasons why, as well as some potential solutions. Have these agents gotten you auditions in the past, with no track record of call-backs on your part? If so, their interest in you may have cooled. Remember, agents have clients of their own to whom they give priority. Another possibility is that these agents haven't seen you—or your work—in too long a period of time. If you suspect that either situation may be the case, discuss with your manager the possibility of remeeting and reauditioning for these agents. If this notion is rejected by your manager or by the agents themselves, consider the possibility of trying to meet more agents.

Here is what to do. Ask your manager to do a mailing of your photo and resume to any agents with whom he or she does *not* have a relationship. If your photo and resume spark interest, your manager will hear from the agents who want to meet you. Although agents often contend otherwise, most of them are willing to work with personal managers provided that the manager is reputable, and, of course, represents a client or clients whom the agent feels are worth an investment. If for any reason your manager is reluctant to do this or fails to act on your request, say that *you* will be willing to do the mailing. Bring in the list of agents you choose to contact and ask for your manager's approval. In your cover letter to the agents, be certain to say that you are "available exclusively through my personal manager Elizabeth Roberts at. . . ." Then list your manager's telephone number, not yours.

Next, get your manager's approval of the letter. After all, you are a signed client, and you want to follow proper protocol. If these agents don't respond, you can stay in touch with them by mail—with progress reports—always reminding them that you are available through your personal manager. I've had many actors—and managers—get excellent results with this approach. And if *you* end up as the writer of the letter—as in the latter situation—and this results in creating new business relationships for your manager as well as for yourself, you will also have succeeded in making your manager very happy. (Remember, you've asked me how to *improve* the situation, not end it!)

Part Two:
Working with Agents

By free-lancing with more than one agency for theatrical representation, I assume that I might benefit from the combination of their energies and professional contacts and that I might be submitted for a broader range of roles. Besides these potential advantages, are there other gains to be realized by free-lancing rather than signing?

The advantages you named are desirable, of course, but the free-lance situation doesn't always work out quite so ideally. I suppose, however, one tangible benefit is that—unlike the signed agency client—you will be "cleared" for individual projects as they come up. That is, the agent will call you and ask to be your agent of record for a specific project. Therefore, you can monitor your actual track record as to (1) how often you are being submitted; (2) what you get submitted for; and (3) what percent of these submissions subsequently result in auditions. The signed agency client is not cleared project by project, of course, and therefore tends to be a bit more in the dark—at least in terms of the ratio of submissions as they result in actual auditions.

I am currently free-lancing with three different agencies for theatrical representation. All of them follow the proper procedure of calling to "clear" me—that is, they call and make sure that no other agent has called to submit me for the same project. Still, I've run into a problem. One of the three has the best track record of actually securing auditions for me subsequent to the submission of my photo and resume, but she isn't always the one who calls first to clear me. That is, the other two often call me sooner, but rarely succeed in getting me the auditions. It's tempting, of course, to tell the weaker ones that I've already been cleared and then save myself for agent

**number three, but that doesn't seem right, somehow.
Is there a solution? I know I'm losing auditions.**

Yes, there is a solution. First, you're correct when you say that
it doesn't seem quite right to "save yourself" for agent number three. It's not only improper, but you could easily get
caught if, for example, the first agent who calls is thus far the
only agent in town who knows about the project. Some
agents—suspicious that an actor is being dishonest in this
fashion—have been known to fabricate the name of a nonex-
istent project just to see if perhaps the actor has already been
cleared. If the actor has, the game is over, and so is the relationship.

You don't need any of this, so here is what to do. Call
the agent who is successful in getting you auditions but often
gets to you last when it comes to clearances. Tell her that of
all the agents you are working with, she is the one with the
most clout, and also tell her how much you appreciate what
she has been able to do for you. If you explain your dilemma
and ask if she will work out an arrangement of exclusivity,
she'll most likely help you.

Let's put it this way. If you don't talk to her now, before
long you'll probably go on her back burner because when she
keeps calling to "clear" you, you'll usually already have been
cleared by someone else. Eventually, she's likely to stop calling
altogether, and you may end up getting no auditions at all.

If she offers to sign you or asks you to be exclusive with
her, you'll need to call the other two agents right away.
Thank them for what they've done—after all, they tried—and
then tell them that one of the other agents with whom
you've been free-lancing has offered to sign you or has offered
you an agreement of exclusivity, whichever it may be, and
that you have accepted her offer. These other agents may not
like your decision, but you are in business for yourself, and
therefore you must act in *your* best interest.

I currently have a free-lance relationship with an agent whom I'll call Agent A. Although I don't hear from her very often, she always calls to clear me when she is working on a project that she feels I might be suited for. I've just met and auditioned for another agent, Agent B, who wants to start working with me as well. I'm certain they'll both be calling to clear me for at least some of the same projects in the near future. So Agent A will, at times, now be competing to clear me—something she and I haven't had to deal with until now. My question is this: When do I tell her? Now? Or when she calls to clear me and I have to tell her that another agent has already called?

Your first guess is the correct one—tell her *now.* Call Agent A and say that you appreciate the auditions she has gotten for you and that you would like to continue working with her. Tell her that another agent has also expressed interest in free-lancing with you, and that you wanted to let her know right away to avoid any confusion or problems. The second possibility that you outlined—waiting until such time as Agent A calls and you must decline a clearance because Agent B has beat her to it, thereby informing her that you are also working with another agent—is most unwise. This approach invariably brings a response such as, "Well, why didn't you tell me you were working with another agent? You should *always* tell any other agents you're working with about any other agents, etc. etc., etc." You see, if an agent presumes she's the only agent you're working with, she'll sometimes be slow on calling to clear you simply because she assumes there will be no problem. Suddenly, when presented with one, she'll hit the roof—and that you can bank on. Unfortunately, actors usually learn this protocol the hard way. And it happens all the time. (Now, tell me honestly, don't you think the *business* of acting is really *fun?*)

I've been free-lancing with an agent for several months. Since I'm not getting very many auditions, I have just met with another agent who would also like to work with me. It seems as though Agent #1 is well aware of the fact that up until now I haven't been working with any other agents, because she no longer bothers to clear me. I don't want to cause any problems with either agent. What is the best way to handle this situation?

Your situations differs from the one above in that you have said that your agent no longer bothers to clear you. Therefore, in similar fashion to the preceding situation, call Agent #1 immediately to say that you want to continue working with her and that you appreciate the activity that she has gotten for you so far. Then tell her that another agent has also expressed interest in free-lancing with you, and you would appreciate it if she'd be certain to clear you on all future projects so there will be no confusion for all parties concerned. In doing this, you are simply requesting that proper procedure be observed.

I am presently free-lancing with an agency for theatrical representation. They occasionally have auditions for me, but these are few and far between. The response from casting directors has generally been favorable, and I've gotten called back on at least a few occasions. Besides communicating about specific projects, which I already do, I'm wondering if you can suggest any ideas as to how I can strengthen my relationship with this agency.

There is something you can do that may not strengthen your relationship with this particular agency, but it can certainly help you to establish what may become even better relationships with some others. It's not unlike the "marrying up" strategy with theater companies that I described a while back. This is the "talent agency" version of the same idea.

You mentioned that you occasionally get called back on the auditions this agency gets for you. I have a question. When you do get a call-back, do you report that to all other agents with whom you might also like to work? What I'm getting at is this. Actors often put enormous energy into trying to get more activity from a particular agent or agency than this individual or outfit has to give them. For whatever unknown reason, this particular agency does not have a great deal of activity for you. And because you have a free-lance relationship with this agency, there has been no commitment on their part to help you find work. What that also means, of course, is that there is no commitment on *your* part to work exclusively with *them*. And *that* means you owe it to *yourself* to keep up the search for the best representation you can find! Therefore, every time you get a call-back from an audition that this agent gets for you, be sure to send postcards to any and all other agents you would like to meet. It's not necessary to mention on the postcard the name of the agent or agency who sent you on the audition; you can always tell them when they ask.

This can be a real door-opener and start to snowball your agency contacts. What you are doing here is pumping out to other agents the good response you are getting as a result of your current free-lance relationship. This plan of attack is *only* for free-lancers. If you are presently *signed* with an agency, you already have a commitment.

I've often heard agents say that a signed contract or commitment between an actor and an agent is like a marriage. Is that an accurate description of the agent/actor relationship?

The notion that the agent/actor relationship is like a marriage has always been somewhat irksome to me. If the relationship is "like a marriage," as agents sometimes put it, then I have a question. How is it that you are "married" when agents themselves often have fifty or sixty or more other clients? That is, you're "married" to them, but they are also "married" to scores of others? Something seems out of whack here.

I also think this notion can set the actor up with some highly unrealistic expectations. In other words, if they've told you that you are "married," then it would be logical to assume that they will share the burden of your career responsibilities—and ideally, they will, at least to *some* degree. But all this can make actors feel that they're off the hook as far as being accountable for their own careers.

The term "married" can also potentially intimidate actors into thinking that they should not consider moving on when the relationship is no longer viable. (At least, that's what married *used* to mean!) Rather, I believe that actors should think of the agent/actor relationship as a business arrangement between two parties who, by contractual agreement and for a specified period of time, will work and communicate with each other unless the relationship proves not to be productive for either or both parties. Remember, agency contracts are union sanctioned, and therefore, the terms of them lean largely in the actor's favor. They are easily dissoluble by either party if the actor is unable to attain work. Some marriage, eh?

I've just started to audition for television commercials, and I am now free-lancing with two different commercial agencies. Neither of them ever calls to clear me. One—or the other—just calls with an audition appointment. What gives?

What gives is that the policy of clearing free-lance talent for submission is simply not observed in the commercial world as it is in the theatrical world. As I mentioned earlier, when a commercial casting director phones a breakdown to a commercial agent, the agent gives the casting director a list of names. Therefore, if your name has *already* been submitted by Agent A, the casting director will inform Agent B of this fact when Agent B attempts to submit you for the very same commercial: "Thank you, but Bob has already been submitted by another agent."

I have free-lanced with several agencies in the past— with results ranging from disappointing to moderately satisfactory. I have an interview pending with an agency, and if they propose an offer to free-lance, I'm inclined to say that I'm only interested in a relationship as a signed client at this point in time. Would this approach be a wise one?

Not unless you're prepared for one of the following outcomes: (1) Resentment on the part of the agent because you've asked for more than they have offered, which possibly could result in diminished interest in you. (2) A change on their part from a free-lance offer to a signed agreement as you requested, but simply to appease you and without any added interest. That is, if they would like to work with you and they think you'll *feel better* being signed, they might go along with it—but it doesn't mean they'll put one more iota of steam into your career than they would have if you were just free-lancing. (3) An offer to sign you because they were afraid you'd say you only wanted to free-lance if *they'd* asked *you* to sign first. (Possible, but not likely.) (4) An offer to sign you due to heightened respect for your assertiveness. (You can pretty much forget about this one.)

It is generally my policy merely to analyze situations and point out options rather than to give advice, but the word from here is to accept what they offer and see where the relationship takes you. That is, unless you're willing to jeopardize your chances of working with them altogether. Remember, putting your name on a piece of paper such as a contract in situations like this one means little more than just that—your name on a piece of paper.

Several months ago, I signed with an agency for the-atrical representation. However, I have only been sent out on a handful of auditions since then. I've noticed friends of mine getting auditions through their agents for things I think I should be seen for as well. I haven't really said much to my agent yet, and I'm wondering what is the best way to handle this frustrating situation.

It's really time for communication. Unfortunately, many actors keep this waiting syndrome going for too long and then have a blowout of sorts with their agent. Let's take measures to avoid that. Here is what to do.

Call your agent and tell her that you would like to speak with her for a few minutes—either on the phone or in person—and ask when would be a good time for her. Be prepared that "a good time" might be right then; this request sometimes makes agents anxious, and they want to attend to it right away. For this reason, I suggest avoiding—at this point in your relationship, anyway—telling your agent that you'd like to have a *meeting* with her.

At the appointed time—whenever it may be—start by letting your agent know that you appreciate the auditions she's gotten for you thus far. That is, keep any reference to your working relationship in the *present* lest she think you are speaking with her to terminate it. Sincerely thank her, then, for her efforts on your behalf. After all, you really don't know yet why she hasn't been able to do more, and her reasons may well be legitimate. Tell her that, of course, you'd like to be auditioning more, and that you have heard about a few projects that you thought you were suited for in the recent past. Be prepared to give your agent specifics, because you will probably be asked for them.

Your agent's response is of critical importance here, and you should listen to it carefully. If she says that in the future you should call her at the time you hear about the project (and not after the fact), and that she will do everything she can to get you seen, fine. You're well on the way to establishing a far better working relationship, and you will know that your communication is welcomed.

However, it is possible that she will say something like this: "The reason you weren't seen for the NBC series 'Such and Such' is because the casting director, So-and-So, felt that you were too young [or too old!] for the role of the star's brother." "The reason you weren't seen for the other project you mentioned, 'What's It Called?' was because the casting director, What's-His-Name, thinks you're too waspy and upscale, and they were looking for someone more 'street' or 'blue-collar.' [Or once again, vice-versa!] As you may know, Al James got the role—so you can see the direction they were looking in." If this is the response, you know your agent is trying, and she's following up on her submissions by actually discussing you with the casting director. It's very important that you know that.

On the other hand, if your agent is vague in her response when you discuss specific projects, such as, "I'm really not sure why you weren't seen for that, but you were submitted"; or, "Well, I'm submitting you on everything, but they just don't seem to be biting . . ."; then ask if the casting directors are saying anything about you—or perhaps about your photo and resume—*when the agent speaks to them about you*. Again, your agent's response is of critical importance because in listening to it, you will know whether or not she is actually following up after she submits you.

In either case, if you want to improve your situation with your agent, do the following. Ask your agent if there is anything *you* can do to make her job easier; in other words, can you meet her part way? Here are some possible ideas for you to suggest: Are your photos all that they should be? Could you revamp your resume to market yourself more effectively? Should you be showcasing more often? Should you be dropping a line to casting directors more often to let them know your progress? Be aware that it is not uncommon for agents to say, "No, don't worry about doing anything. I'll take care of all the business aspects. That's *my* job." It's well intentioned, of course, but it can be hazardous.

There's an old saw in the business that goes, "Actors are 90 percent responsible for their careers, and agents are only 10 percent responsible, because that's the percentage they get." I'll take that one step further: Actors are 100 percent responsible for their careers. Therefore, I think you should consider all of the above suggestions as possible improvements—just be sure to discuss them with your agent first. Again, be certain to keep your communication about projects that are happening *current*—don't wait until after it's too late (see *AAB*, pp. 71–86). If your relationship with your agent doesn't improve, if you've communicated specifically, diplomatically, and to the best of your ability, and if you still feel that you can do better with respect to representation, then read on.

I have been signed with an agency for the past year, and I'm certain that there are more auditions I could be getting. Although I haven't landed a job, I've gotten called back on several of the auditions I've had. I know my agent likes me, and I feel sure she's going to ask me to re-sign when my contracts expire in a couple of weeks. However, with my current track record of so few auditions, I'd like to explore other options for representation. At the same time, I don't want to be left without an agent. How do I protect my interests and at the same time do what's right? I've communicated throughout the relationship to the very

best of my ability, and my agent knows that I'm not especially satisfied.

Here are your options—outlining both the possible benefits as well as the risks. Since your agency contracts are on the verge of expiration, you can send your photo and resume along with a cover letter to any other agents you would like to meet. A possible benefit is, of course, that you might get a great new agent who is able to provide you with many more audition opportunities than your present agent can. The obvious risk in signing with a new agent who looks promising is that you may end up in a situation that is no better than your current one. In fact, it could turn out to be even worse.

It could also happen that your present agent might learn that you are "looking around"—which is, of course, your right since your contracts are up for renewal. (Instead of viewing the renewal as a mutual decision, agents often treat actors as though the re-signing of contracts is a forgone conclusion: "Bring in some more pictures this week, and by the way, your new contracts are prepared and you can sign them when you stop by.") In any case, should your agent happen to learn that you're "looking around," one of three things is likely to happen: (1) It could make her more eager to improve the situation if she truly wants and values you as a client and is indeed planning to ask you to re-sign. (2) She may tell you that if you feel that someone else can do better for you, you are free to leave. (3) She may ask you to stay with her—if only on a freelance basis. While this third possibility would clearly allow you to seek other representation without "losing" your present agent, there is a built-in risk with this arrangement. Since you would no longer be a "signed" client of your present agent, you could end up on the back burner and find yourself with even fewer auditions than you're getting now—possibly with no new agents showing interest.

Let's look at another option. You could wait and see if, in fact, your present agent does ask you to re-sign, and if she does, you could ask her for a free-lance arrangement instead of a signed agreement. The benefit here would be that you could then start your search for other representation. The risk is essentially the same as in the previous situation: ending up on the back burner. The difference here would be that, unlike option one, your present agent would be aware upfront that you are exploring your options where representation is concerned.

Now, it is possible that your present agent will say no to your request to free-lance, in which case you will be left with two choices: to re-sign or not! All of this without having begun the search for other representation!

Understandably, you say that you are afraid of being without representation. Therefore, your final option is to consider re-signing with your present agent—if asked—without having investigated other options first. I would consider this last option *only* after you: thank your agent for what she has been able to do for you; tell her that you are willing to recommit; and then tell her, precisely and nicely, the areas in which you would like to see improvements made. *Listen to what your agent has to say.* If she feels certain she can and will be able to do more, and you feel that this is your safest and best option, then re-sign with your present agent. The risk here is, of course, that there might be someone else out there *now* who indeed would be better for you. However, if you do re-sign and no improvements are forthcoming, you can exercise the "out" clause detailed in your agency contract and be free of your present agent altogether.

The point of all of this is to get you to analyze the risk factors in your career decision-making. Ask yourself, What is the *best* thing that could happen? (I could get a great new agent.) What is the *worst* thing that could happen? (I could be left with no agent at all.) Therefore, in choosing any option discussed here, remember: If you can't accept the worst, *don't do it.*

Part Three:
More About Soaps

I recently attended a seminar that was conducted by an assistant casting director of a daytime soap opera. He acknowledged that he looks at postcards and responds to them, but he advised us that sending one postcard per month was sufficient. He said he doesn't need a card every week. Yet, in *Acting As a Business* [pp. 33–37], you said that sending a postcard weekly to the soaps was an actor's best bet. Which do you think is better? Once a week? Or once a month?

Once a week—although the casting director was telling the absolute truth when he said he doesn't need a weekly card from you. I'll go one better. He doesn't *ever* need a postcard from you. He gets more than enough as it is. You see, each soap gets hundreds of pieces of mail each week. That is, they get mail from every actor who would like to work for them, as well as from the many actors who have *already* worked for them and want to work for them again. Throwing modesty aside, daytime television is an area of the industry in which I have helped thousands of actors find employment. My observation over the years is this. Actors who write once a week usually work. Those who write once a month usually don't. Sometimes an actor will say to me, "I've been writing to the soaps for eight months and haven't heard anything." And I say, "How often do you write?" Common answer: "Once a month." In a case such as this, the actor would be represented by exactly *eight* pieces of mail in anywhere from ten thousand to twenty thousand at each soap!

However, if you write once a week, you simply increase your chances. So then, in a year's time, it is better to be represented by fifty-two pieces of mail than by twelve! A basic tenet of good marketing and advertising—in any business—is repetition. Casting directors need to see your name, face, and credibility-building message with frequency, or they'll just be less inclined to think of you. In fact, former soap casting directors, *no longer bombarded by enormous volumes of mail them-selves,* generally recommend the "once a week" approach.

This entire discussion makes me feel it is necessary to talk about another element at work here. While I believe that most casting directors and agents who are guests at seminars are genuinely trying to give helpful information to the partic-ipating actor, they often feel a need to protect themselves at the same time. So a dual message goes out. On the one hand, they are telling you to be persistent. On the other hand, *they're keeping you at bay.* If I presently held the job of casting director or agent, my perspective would probably be the same as theirs—and I would most likely say the things that they do without really thinking about the whole picture. But I no longer have that job. I have *this* job. Which is to tell you that my twenty years of observation convince me that writing to a soap once a month isn't sufficient. Okay, enough said. You've heard it from all sides now. *You* decide.

Since soaps air five days a week, fifty-two weeks a year, and therefore aren't on the same shoot schedule as prime-time shows, are there any specific times of the year when an actor's chances of getting work are better than at others?

I would say that a very young—or at least very young-*looking*—actor who can still play teenage roles has an increased chance of getting work in the summer, when soap writers put strong emphasis on their high school/college-age characters and story lines. Why is this? Well, school's out, and the soaps want to boost that age demographic in their viewership.

Also, any actor who is contacting soaps by mail on a regular basis should keep a sharp eye out for changes in soap opera assistant—or associate—casting directors. This informa-tion will be listed in *Ross Reports Television* as well as on the AFTRA hotlines in both New York and Los Angeles. A photo and resume sent *immediately* when a new assistant or associate casting director at a soap opera is assigned—followed up by a telephone call seeking an interview—can be highly effective. When new assistants are hired at a soap, they almost always set up interviews with actors in order to build or expand their files. If you are fortunate enough to get work right after this casting director has begun his or her new job, it's not usually too difficult to get a good amount of work from them in the future since you got in with them at the beginning. Important: Casting personnel will almost always discourage telephone calls from actors. *They have to.* But I have observed that a well-placed follow-up phone call *immediately* after a change of assistant casting director at a soap very often results in an interview. Do I feel like I'm declaring open season on my friends in casting? Not at all. No matter how often I say this, it will still be the rare actor who is really on top of this situation or who bothers to act on it with the necessary immediacy.

I have an appointment scheduled for a general interview at a soap opera. Is it possible that I will also be asked to audition at that time?

It's *very* possible. Some casting people at soaps give the actor "sides" to read from—a scene—from a past or future episode of the soap. They may even give you a sample scene that they use for general interviews or auditions. Others may ask you to perform a monologue.

Asking the actor to read a scene or perform a monologue helps the casting person get a sense of the actor's overall potential. Also, some soap casting personnel won't even put an actor on the set as an extra *without* first having heard a reading or monologue. Their feeling is that if the actor should be upgraded to a small speaking role or "under-five," which commonly happens, but can't handle it, it makes *them* look bad for having hired this actor in the first place. Some soaps observe this policy strictly; others wing it a bit. In any case, *always be prepared to audition.*

Do you know of any sources of information for discovering current and upcoming casting on soap operas?

Yes. AFTRA hotlines in both New York and Los Angeles give soap casting information in addition to the updated changes in soap opera casting personnel mentioned earlier. Largely, this information is limited to minor and recurring roles. *Soap Opera Weekly,* a consumer periodical (see Appendix D), often features in its weekly column "Revolving Door" a category entitled "Watch For." This section regularly features tips concerning current and upcoming soap casting—the extent of which depends upon what's happening in the soap world. At times, then, this information will be more plentiful than at others. Often, new roles are described in relationship to existing roles, so a knowledge of current soap characters is helpful.

These tips can best be used to alert an agent, but I have known actors without representation to get results as well. If you are in the latter category and are pursuing work in daytime television, here is what to do. When you learn of a role for which you feel you may be suited, send your photo and resume along with a typed cover letter (of course!) to the head casting director of the soap.

Let me throw in a general rule here, one that goes beyond soaps. When contacting a casting director (or director, producer, etc.) about a role in a specific project, always apprise the reader of this in the very first sentence of your cover letter. In this case, your first sentence after "Dear Mr. [or Ms.] _____" should read, "Enclosed is my photo and resume for the upcoming role of Adam Buckley on *Guiding Light.*"

The body of your letter should be brief, and depending upon what's presently happening in your career, might follow along the lines of the sample cover letter in *Acting As a Business* (p. 34). You should also mention any impressive and recent callbacks you've gotten—especially if they were for roles on other soaps.

After putting your photo, resume, and cover letter in a manila envelope, mark the lower left-hand corner of the envelope with the name of the character: "Re: Adam Buckley role." I recommend *only* a mail-in approach here—no phone follow-up. If they're interested, you'll hear from them.

After writing to the soaps for several months requesting a general audition, I telephoned and got through to a couple of the assistant casting directors. One of them suggested that I "try back in about a month," which I did. At that point he suggested that I try back once again "in about a month." Is there an effective way to handle a situation like this when someone keeps telling you to "try back"?

Yes, there is—and this suggestion can be used in any situation where this happens, not just soaps. When someone invites you to "try again," make sure that when you do, you start your conversation by giving your name and then saying, *"When I last spoke with you on May 3rd,* you suggested that I try you again in about a month. So I wanted to get back to you and see if perhaps we could arrange an interview." *Give them the date* of your last conversation. It lets them know *what* they said and *when* they said it. It's properly assertive, businesslike, and your call will be taken more seriously. Also, it's highly unlikely that you would be asked to "try again" if this person wasn't sincere. If he didn't want you to call, he'd tell you.

I am constantly being told that I resemble one of the stars of a popular soap opera. Do you think that if I

submit my photo and resume along with a letter pointing this out, then they would consider creating a role as this character's brother?

Probably not unless they are *already* planning to create or cast this role to begin with! What I mean is this. The writers would be more likely to create the character of "the brother" *first*, and *then* go looking for an actor who might bear physical resemblance to the first actor (rather than the other way around). They wouldn't be likely to create a character—and the whole story line that goes with it—simply because there is an actor out there who resembles the first actor. But, by all means, send your photo and resume to the casting office on the off chance that they do indeed create this character or in the more likely event that they may want to use you for something else.

I have had a contract role on a New York soap opera for the past two years. I like the security and the salary, but I don't want to get stuck here. What can I do to use this job as a springboard for bigger things?

This is really an important time to have a meeting with your agent to discuss your career goals. One common syndrome for an actor in your situation is for your agent to think of you as being "taken care of for now" since you already have a steady job. Also, the way you are perceived by your agent can determine how much he or she is actually thinking about you at this time. Your agent may think you are a terrific actor with great potential for bigger things—and it so happens that a soap is where you landed first. *Or,* your agent may have initially taken you on as a client thinking, "This guy will probably be able to get a soap."

If you suspect that you are perceived as being in the latter category, you may really need to assert yourself to have your ambitions made known and realized. In any case, it would be wise to get in a good acting class (if you aren't already in one) so that you're not just cranking out that one character you've been playing day after day. Also, check your soap contract to see what kind of a break you can get for short-term work on a film or, perhaps, for other television work. Be sure to bring this temporary "out" clause to your agent's attention. In addition, enlist your agent's help and try to get yourself in a play. The theater is where a lot of industry people who are currently *not* paying attention to you will have the opportunity to discover who you are.

In any case, this is an important time in your young career to use your time and energies well. The notion of getting "stuck" on a soap opera is, in reality, a rather exaggerated fear that actors have. The overwhelming majority of young actors who land a contract role on a soap do not end up getting "stuck" there. They get written off the show. (And very often wish they *had* gotten "stuck" there!)

As a contract player on a soap opera, I'm wondering if this status will give me a competitive edge for theater work in New York. It seems like there has been an influx of soap actors both on and off Broadway lately.

There is really nothing new about actors on soaps working simultaneously in the New York theater—either on Broadway or off. Historically, many, many actors under contract on a soap opera have also worked on or off Broadway at the same time they were appearing on the soap. In fact, it has typically been the so-called "soap" actor's *stage* career—not soap career—that has actually launched a bigger career in film or prime-time television.

In general, working in daytime television was—and is— a job that few New York actors are in a financial position not to accept, even if they don't necessarily consider it their dream acting job. That is, many of these actors aren't "soap" actors at all. Rather, they are *actors* who happen to be on a soap. Let's take a look back over the years at some of the New York actors who played major roles on soaps and also worked on the stage. A partial list includes: Lee Grant, Warren Beatty, Don Knotts (!), Hal Holbrook, Sandy Dennis, Rue McClanahan, Ellen Burstyn, Roy Scheider, Robert DeNiro, Jill Clayburgh, Patty Duke, James Earl Jones, Billy Dee Williams, Martin Sheen, Dick Van Patten, Peter Falk, Kathy Bates, Cicely Tyson, Larry Hagman, Barnard Hughes, Frances Sternhagen, Ted Danson, Kathleen Turner, Christopher Reeve, Kevin Bacon, Sigourney Weaver, JoBeth Williams, Tommy Lee Jones, Christine Ebersole, Julianne Moore, Laurence Fishburne, Ray Liotta, Lynne Thigpen, Morgan Freeman, Robert Loggia, Bonnie Bedelia, Judith Light, Ann Wedgeworth, Dixie Carter, Peter Gallagher, Steven Weber, Armand Assante, Dana Delaney, Olympia Dukakis, Ian Ziering, Christian Slater, Josh Hamilton, Giancarlo Esposito, and on and on. Interestingly, in the past, an actor's soap career was rarely, if ever, considered a catalyst to his or her stage career. Yet so-called "soap" actors who are, today, also appearing on or off Broadway find that their soap jobs now get the credit for landing them the stage gigs. This notion is not entirely accurate, and, in fact, is often downright false.

What, then, changed this perception? Certainly one event contributed to it greatly. In 1993, Andrew Lloyd Webber and The Really Useful Theater Company announced that Michael Damian would star in a revival of *Joseph and the Amazing Technicolor Dreamcoat*. What was unprecedented here was that the star of a *Los Angeles* daytime soap opera was now going to star in a Broadway production! And since actors from prime-time television series have clout in the New York theater (which is often how they landed the prime-time series to begin with), the popular sentiment became, "Well, I guess if you're even on a *soap* these days, you get to star on Broadway!"

Well, not quite. Reality check: Michael Damian was not just an "actor on a soap." He had—since 1981—been one of the stars of the consistently Number One rated daytime soap opera on the air—CBS' *The Young and the Restless*. His soap career had come as a direct result of his singing career, which not only *preceded* his soap career—it was the very reason for it. In 1980, after having performed for several years with his family, Mr. Damian struck out on his own and cut his first solo recording. As a result, he appeared on *American Bandstand*, where he was seen by the producers of *The Young and the Restless*, who decided to create a pop-rock singer as a character on their show. Mr. Damian's soap career and his music career became intertwined, and several hit records followed, including the Billboard Hot 100 Number One hit "Rock On."

Michael Damian was not only *not* just an "actor on a soap," he wasn't even a "soap star"—a term that seems to get handed out generically to every actor who has a soap opera contract. Indeed, Mr. Damian was a bona fide soap opera *superstar*, as well as being one of perhaps only three daytime television actors known to the American public by their *real* name—Susan Lucci and Anthony Geary being the others. What's more, it was written into *The Young and the Restless* storyline that Damian's TV character, pop-rock singer Danny Romalotti, had been cast in the title role of the revival of *Joseph!* This meant that nearly seven million viewers watched on a daily basis as Damian/Romalotti went through the paces of rehearsals, the successful Los Angeles run of *Joseph*, and then its preparation for Broadway. This publicity machine— which included Damian frequently performing numbers from *Joseph* on the soap—helped drum up a strong box office advance and, indeed, helped to keep *Joseph* running for many more months than had originally been planned. Incidentally, it also kept approximately thirty other actors employed! (Not including the children's chorus.)

In addition to having a pop-rock score, *Joseph* was a revival, which typically requires a "name" actor to begin with, and with a plot based on a character from the Bible, it was a show that was definitely fare for "the entire family."

This revival, then, yearned for a popular young actor/singer with a following and the required discipline to perform eight exhausting shows each week. With *twelve years* of experience co-starring on the top-rated daytime serial on the air *and* a highly successful international recording and concert career to boot, Michael Damian was, at thirty, an ideal candidate for *Joseph*. But just an "actor on a soap"? Well, no.

Immediately thereafter, actor Ricky Paull Goldin, who was also playing a pop singer on a soap opera—Dean Frame on NBC's *Another World*—was cast as Danny Zuko opposite Rosie O'Donnell in the Broadway revival of *Grease!* Well, now it just had to be that "soap actors" were taking over Broadway! But what many people didn't realize was that long before becoming a "soap actor," a very young Ricky Paull Goldin had made his Broadway debut years earlier as the flippant thirteen-year-old Billy Ray in *On Golden Pond*. Just a child then, Goldin also had appeared in the London production of the Broadway hit *The Magic Show;* later would work with The New York Shakespeare Festival, also as a regular on a prime-time television series and in feature films as well—all prior to his gig on *Another World*. A "soap actor"? Not exactly!

Sure enough, at approximately the very same time, another young actor, Paul Anthony Stewart of the soap opera formerly known as *Loving* (now called *The City*), landed the role of Christian in a new Broadway production entitled *Cyrano, the Musical*. Although this was Mr. Stewart's Broadway debut, a look at his resume tells us that he had already performed major roles in nearly fifty stage productions—a number of them at prestigious Equity regional and New York theaters.

And so it went, while the media pumped out stories about "Soap Opera Stars On Broadway!" Ironically, the very same articles could have been written ten, twenty, thirty, and even forty years ago simply by changing the names of the actors and the titles of the shows! Interesting, too, was that at about this very same time, a couple of producers, in an apparent attempt to cash in on what appeared to be a new trend, hired other popular soap stars—and I do mean "soap stars": multi-Daytime-Emmy-Award-winning actors with a decade or more experience on soaps—as cast replacements in New York productions. Unfortunately, the stage background of these actors was little, or long ago, or else the productions they were hired for were not of a mainstream variety likely to attract soap viewers. In each case, the producers found themselves posting closing notices within weeks.

I would say, then, that an actor on a soap has to be more that just a "soap actor" to be taken seriously in the New York theater. At least, let's *hope* so! If this were not the case, we'd be seeing many more actors from soaps on the stage than we do; these actors know, career-wise, that the stage is potentially their ticket to bigger and better things, yet only a small percentage of them are actually landing these stage jobs. And, despite the way it may *seem,* far more theater jobs still lead to soap jobs than the other way around. Remember, when an actor's visibility in a play leads to a soap job, we don't hear about it. But when a soap job leads to a theater job, it generates publicity because the soap has millions more viewers than the play will ever have! Hence, stories appear in the media—designed, of course, to generate ticket sales.

Recently, Jeff Trachta, star of the L.A. soap *The Bold and the Beautiful,* made a highly publicized debut on Broadway as a cast replacement in the revival of *Grease!* Originally a New York actor with highly impressive theater credits, it was unsurprising to hear Trachta say that it was actually his visibility in a *stage* production in L.A. that brought about his Broadway engagement in *Grease!*

All told, your soap status offers no guarantee of entree into theatrical circles, but it can certainly help since television, in general, offers more credibility as a conduit to other areas of the industry than it once did. Also, the general perception is that actors on New York soaps are not only attractive, but they can also act, and—in the right vehicle at least—*they can attract ticket buyers.* Therefore, you should do all that you can to use your current situation to further your career.

Like the actor in the preceding situation, you should have a serious meeting with your agent and map out all your possibilities. You really have the right to expect cooperation here; after all, you're paying your agency a hefty commission on a weekly basis. If cooperation is not forthcoming, take matters into your hands and approach casting directors on your own, using the methods outlined in *Acting As a Business* (pp. 71–86).

Part Four:
From Stage to Screen:
Revisited

My background is musical theater. As a strong singer and dancer, I really want to expand my possibilities and cross over into an acting career in television or film. I feel that I've been pigeonholed, and I'm told that it will be hard to get industry people to change their perception of me. What means can I take to be seriously considered for work that is nonmusical?

You are probably pretty much on the money when you say that you've gotten "pigeonholed," and yet it's important to realize that the reason for this is because the area you've been trained in and have worked in has been musical theater. So it's really only natural that casting directors, directors, agents etc., think of you for this kind of work. However, some musical theater artists do cross over into "straight" acting careers, either on stage or in film and television. Of the latter two, it is particularly the case with television, where the continual demand for new, fresh, and ongoing programming potentially allows for the highly visible (and fortunate) stage performer to enter the ranks of the rich and the famous.

What enables musical theater performers to make a crossover has a great deal to do with the very nature of the specific musicals in which they are seen—and, of course, the level of visibility of the productions themselves. Some musicals are viewed as "singers' musicals," or even "song and dance musicals," and still others are considered "actors' musicals." I don't mean that people necessarily categorize consciously in this way, but the way a performer is perceived—and therefore considered for work in other areas of the industry besides musical theater—will often be dictated by these factors.

Okay, so what would be considered a "singers' musical"? *Les Miserables, Phantom of the Opera,* and *Miss Saigon* are a few examples of what I would call "singers' musicals." The primary emphasis in each is on the vocal. "Song and dance musicals" would include shows such as *Cats* and *A Chorus Line.* Notice that few performers from these Broadway productions have gone on to major careers in film or television, *unless* they later appeared in musicals that showcased them as *actors*—not just as singer/dancers. Case in point: Bebe Neuwirth, who appeared in New York sketch revues as well as on Broadway in such productions as *Dancin'*, *Little Me*, and *A Chorus Line*. However, it was Ms. Neuwirth's Tony Award winning performance as Nickie in the Broadway revival of *Sweet Charity* that made the television industry take note of her talents in a big way. Subsequent to her performance in *Charity*, Ms. Neuwirth landed her two-time Emmy-Award-winning role of Lilith, Frasier's acerbic wife on *Cheers*. Certainly, the character of Nickie had allowed Neuwirth to showcase her strong talents as a comedic actress better than her previous Broadway shows had. And, of course, the Tony didn't hurt either!

Jason Alexander's career came to the forefront following his Tony-Award-winning performance in *Jerome Robbins' Broadway*. While this show would largely be considered a "song and dance" show, it featured Mr. Alexander's comedic talents brilliantly, and within a year *Seinfeld* would follow. John Goodman, still another strong character actor, cites his role as Pap Finn in the 1986 Broadway musical *Big River* (an "actors' musical") as his "Big Break."

In another case, actor/singer Randy Graff, Broadway's original Fantine in *Les Miserables*, was awarded a Tony a few years after *Les Miz* for her work in the Cy Coleman musical *City of Angels* (an "actors' musical"). This production allowed Ms. Graff to show her remarkable skills as a comedic actress, and a short while thereafter, she too became a series regular—on the situation comedy *Drexell's Class*. A few seasons later, Ms. Graff returned to Broadway in a leading role in the new Neil Simon comedy *Laughter on the Twenty-third Floor*, marking her first time on Broadway in a nonmusical role. More recently, she appeared opposite Carol Burnett in another nonmusical role on Broadway in the comedy *Moon Over Buffalo*.

Still another actor, Michael Jeter, fresh from his Tony-Award-winning role in *Grand Hotel, The Musical*—in which he was clearly featured as an *actor*—landed himself a regular role on the series *Evening Shade*. His television career has since led to work in film, as he has played featured and leading roles in such movies as *The Fisher King* and *Waterworld*.

Despite becoming the toast of Broadway in the 1979–80 season for her Tony-winning performance in *Evita* (a "singers' musical"), Patti LuPone made her most significant mark in the film and television industry after she later starred on Broadway as Reno Sweeney in the revival of *Anything Goes*. It didn't hurt matters that Reno was *not* an all-singing role as Evita had been—and a short while thereafter, Ms. LuPone won the starring role in the ABC series *Life Goes On*.

Interestingly, actor/singer Mandy Patinkin—who also won a Tony for *Evita*—was shortly thereafter cast opposite Barbra Streisand in *Yentl*. While Streisand sang throughout the film, Patinkin's audiences waited all during it for him to do the one thing he—ironically—never got around to doing—sing!

Perhaps one of the best examples of an "actors' musical" that launched many a film and television career was the 1970's blockbuster Broadway musical *Grease*. Although the show was a musical, with singing and dancing replete, it equally emphasized characterization and comedy. That is, gorgeous vocal instruments and glorious terpsichorean skills were not requisite attributes for the actors in this show. Indeed, *Grease* was an "actors' musical." Some of its alumni—on Broadway or in national tours and international productions—include John Travolta, Marilu Henner, Patrick Swayze, Barry Bostwick, Peter Gallagher, Richard Gere, Treat Williams, Philip Casnoff, Jeff Conaway, Adrian Zmed, and Adrienne Barbeau.

So there you have a number of actors whose work in *musicals* has led to major careers in television and/or film. In some cases, the actors were cast in film or TV right out of New York. Others—riding the crest of their recent success on the stage and wishing to exploit it fully—departed for Los Angeles, where there are more film and television work opportunities.

Assuming that at the moment you don't happen to have a recent Tony Award sitting on your mantle and that you're not ready to pack up and head for Los Angeles quite yet, here is what to do.

1. Start by taking a good look at your resume. I find that actors are quite clever at resume revamping if they are willing to put the required time and thought into it. Do some of the roles you have played show you off more as an "actor who sings" rather than as a "singer" or a "singer/dancer"? If so, list these credits first on your resume, under the "Theater" category. The order in which you list your credits to catch your reader's eye is a key to self-marketing and affects the way you will be perceived. It's not very likely, however, that you would list an "acting" role at a little-known theater above a "singer" or "singer/dancer" role you may have done on Broadway. That is, make sure you balance your credits in a way that doesn't minimize your accomplishments—or your career level! *Where* you've done what you've done is very important.

2. Get yourself into a good acting class if you aren't already in one. And tell your agent—if you have one—that you are in said class.

3. If you have an agent, enlist his or her aid in your new marketing campaign. Ask your agent to focus more on trying to get you seen for nonmusicals or, at least, for musicals that feature your talents as an *actor* as well. Be prepared that this one might take some time—old prejudices die hard. Ask if you can bring in some monologues to perform for your agent. Be creative in your monologue search. Nonmusical

performers *usually* have a more sophisticated repertoire of monologue material than performers who mainly sing and dance. Don't worry about this. You know more *songs* than they do. That is, you're just used to performing audition material of a very different nature. However, it's very common for a "singer" to pick something really cliche, such as a monologue from *The Glass Menagerie*. This only reinforces the notion that the "singer" probably doesn't spend much time working on or delving into dramatic literature, which is what most *actors* do. (Or *should* do, anyway!)

4. Get yourself in nonmusical showcases around town so that industry people can see you *acting*.

5. If your agent can't get you seen for nonmusical roles (or if you don't have an agent) and you are an "eligible performer," go to EPAs and let casting directors see you performing monologues instead of only singing and dancing. Make *sure* your monologue audition skills are polished first!

6. Consider developing a "one person" show that includes *both* musical and nonmusical material. If you do this, it would be more desirable to perform it in a theater—rather than in a *cabaret* setting. The nature of the venue effects the way in which you are perceived.

7. This option incurs some very great risks—possibly the loss of a lot of income, most likely the wrath of your agent, and absolutely *no* guarantee of results. *Still* care to hear it? Here goes. Accept no further work—or auditions—unless the nature of the production will feature you in the way you wish to be featured. This is what some performers have done—with varying degrees of success. Lynne Thigpen is one performer

who did it successfully. Please understand that this last suggestion is *not* a blithe recommendation; it is an option, and a risky one—it may be that your musical gifts are your strongest suit. However, if you still want to be based in New York and you aspire to a career in film or television, the highest caliber of stage visibility that you can get—in the right kinds of projects—still remains your best bet.

Despite all the examples you've mentioned, wouldn't it be more accurate to say that, on the whole, actors who are *already* names from film and television are now dominating the New York theater scene? Isn't the "stage to screen" connection more or less a thing of the past?

No. On *both* counts. I'll deal with them one at a time in a minute, but first let me say that I'm choosing to address this issue once again because I feel a very strong need to do so. Popular misconception and the media continue to mislead the public—and actors in particular—to believe the notion you have expressed. In *Acting As a Business,* I wrote that fewer than *3 percent* of the performers currently on Equity-salaried contracts—both on Broadway and off—were names from film and television. This same statistic is holding steady at this writing.

Okay, point one. It often *seems* that names from film and television are "dominating" the theater scene for two reasons. (1) *They are the actors whom we are most likely to talk about.* That is, if Kathleen Turner, Carol Burnett, Glenn Close, Dustin Hoffman, Vanessa Redgrave, Matthew Broderick, Julie Andrews, Gene Hackman, or Alec Baldwin are doing a play in New York, it will be highly publicized and, of course, we will talk about it—and them—too. They're stars! What we *won't* talk about—at least until we've seen the production or read reviews of it—are the three or four or eight or ten or forty *others* who will also be in the cast. Why would we talk about them? As often as not, we don't even know who they are. In some cases, however, we soon will. (2) If it *seems* that names from film and television are dominating the theater scene, it is also because disproportionate attention is drawn to the whole matter by those actors who are not in that same league—because they find it so annoying. In fact, Broadway has, for approximately four decades, regularly featured name actors from television. And prior to the invention of television, Broadway regularly featured names from film. Also, in the overwhelming majority of cases, the stars from film and television got into film and television because of their exposure on the stage in the first place. But if you were to take an actual body count—as I have—of actors on and off Broadway, you would see that well over 90 percent of them are *not* names from film and television. And of those who are, most came from the stage in the first place.

So, what really is new? Or at least *newer?* Certainly this. Prior to a few decades ago, if an actor in an off-Broadway production was well-received critically, he or she increased the chances of moving to a career *on* Broadway. From there, the actor had a shot at being picked up by the film and television industry. Off Broadway was considered, at that time, decidedly "less" than Broadway, and rarely did an actor go directly from off Broadway to a career in film or television. And rarely, too, did a "name" actor opt to appear in a production scheduled to play off Broadway. More recently, as the economics of mounting a production on Broadway has resulted in fewer new productions and more revivals, the more serious and even not-so-serious nonmusical new plays are mounted with greater frequency off Broadway, where costs are lower. Therefore, actors now—and for quite some time—have been going directly from off Broadway to film or television careers, and then sometimes they later return to the stage as "stars" and potential sellers of tickets (which is, of course, a big part of the reason they were offered the roles).

Let me illustrate with an example how "the stage to screen" connection sometimes gets lost—whether on Broadway or off—and becomes perceived as "nowadays being the other way around." I recently worked with an actor who told me she had attended a seminar given by a popular television star. He told the group that before becoming famous on TV, he wasn't offered very much in the New York theater. It was only after he became famous that he was able to get the best stage-work. Prior to that, he said, he was only offered smaller roles and understudy work.

I asked the actor if this star had happened to mention that one of his "pre-star" gigs included understudying the star of one of the most successful plays of that time. Apparently he hadn't elaborated to any great degree, and, in not doing so, unintentionally misled the group. The simple fact was that he had performed—as understudy—a lead role in a hit Broadway play *prior* to getting the television series. It was a credit such as this that had actually contributed greatly to his being considered for the series in the first place. The series made him famous and he later came back to Broadway as a *star*.

It is this issue that I find most often escapes the young—and even not-so-young—actor today. Why is this the case? Actors' stage careers are usually far more "low profile" than they once were, when the happenings of the New York theater scene—most commonly Broadway—were pumped to the heart of America. Actors once actually became famous on the stage. What made them famous? Newspapers, magazines, television shows, and radio all carried stories about the newest "Broadway star" or "up-and-coming" young actor. In some cases, of course, these actors were then picked up by Hollywood.

What, specifically, did the media offer then, that it no longer offers, that made the unknown stage actor famous?

Nationally syndicated columns by the likes of such journalists as Dorothy Kilgallen, Walter Winchell, and Earl Wilson, for example, who reported the Broadway happenings on a daily basis—right down to which actors were dating each other. Hard to believe today, but true nonetheless. I recently picked up a copy of *Life* magazine from the fall of 1963. Its cover featured the first new Broadway star of the season—twenty-three-year-old Elizabeth Ashley, who had just opened in Neil Simon's smash hit comedy *Barefoot in the Park*. Commonplace then, it wouldn't happen today. The national media, which once publicized and glamorized the New York theater scene, no longer does. Why not? One reason is that despite the current proliferation of entertainment-oriented publications and entertainment "news" programs, the "entertainment industry" has, as I mentioned earlier, become increasingly multifaceted, and the happenings of the New York theater scene are simply no longer considered to be of great interest to the public at large. After all, most of the time, the performers who are dominating the scene *aren't* well known! And only when they are *already* famous does a magazine, talk show, entertainment program, or newspaper column usually spend any time talking about them—further reinforcing the notion that only actors who are already famous are dominating the New York theater scene!

Okay, what else contributed to the demise of the once famous New York theater scene? Another major factor was the loss of all the New York television variety shows that mainlined both the Broadway music—and the people who made it—to the heartland of America. Such staples as *The Ed Sullivan Show, The Tonight Show, The Garry Moore Show, The Jack Paar Show, and The Merv Griffin Show*—among others—all once emanated from New York City. These variety and talk shows largely featured New York talent. Not only did they present musical performers in great supply, but nonmusical performers were regularly featured guests on these shows as well. These programs provided a showcase for all of America to see, and they made many an up-and-coming stage performer *very* famous.

Not only did the public catch the New York performers through the nightly talk and variety shows, but America got a good steady dose of the New York actor by *day* too! Throughout the 1950s, '60s, and even into the '70s, the New York daytime game shows, of which there were many, featured as "team captains" and hosts—guess who? The Broadway people! All, of course, telling the public about the new play or musical in which they were now appearing. Think of the power of this daily and nightly national advertising for the New York entertainment scene! Hard to imagine, no? If I hadn't lived through it, I don't think I could even conceive of it, but that's the way it was.

Okay, what else was different then? Here comes a *big* one. *Music.* During the 1960s the popular music of the day became more and more youth oriented, with rock music taking an even stronger foothold than it had in the 1950s, and "show tunes" and "original cast recordings" started to become more scarce on the charts and on the airwaves. Not so many years before, the music that parents and their children listened to had actually been the very same. And what music was that? Much of the popular music that was recorded and played on the radio had come from the hit Broadway shows of the day.

And so, in those days, Broadway, music, and the media—print, radio, and television—all fed one another in great supply. But as the costs of production for Broadway escalated—resulting in fewer properties being produced—more and more New York actors headed west, where the land of film and television offered greater possibilities of employment. By this point in time, the economics and logistics of film and television production had become far more attractive and viable in L.A. than in New York. All told, the New York-based television variety and talk shows had little choice but to move west too, as L.A. was where so many guests that would interest the public—stars from film and television—could now be found. As a result, the connection between the New York theater scene and the American public was critically severed—and New York theater performers rarely became showcased on national television. The publicity this once generated had, of course, resulted in gargantuan ticket sales. Still wishing for "names" who could sell tickets, New York theater producers now had to rely on another kind of television. Prime-time dramatic performers and comedy series actors, as well as names from film—most of whom had gotten their start on the stage—were invited to return with increasing frequency. Of course, with even fewer major productions being mounted in New York these days—and with smaller casts (also dictated by economics)—the presence of the stars has become more noticeable than ever.

What about the trend of recording artists—Jon Secada, Sheena Easton, Vanessa Williams, Mac Davis, Petula Clark, Carole King, and Helen Reddy, for example—who come to Broadway *already* famous? Isn't this new?

Not exactly, although we've seen more of it lately than ever. If it seems new, it has to do—once again—with the ways in which both the industry and music itself have changed. For example, many think that the 1964 Broadway musical *Funny Girl* made Barbra Streisand famous. Unarguably, *Funny Girl* made Ms. Streisand a *star*, but she was already famous by the time she appeared in that production. Although she was, as she herself has always contended, "an actress who sings," a previous Broadway appearance in *I Can Get It for You Wholesale*, along with her notoriety on the nightclub circuit, had led to many national television appearances as a vocal artist on such variety programs of the day as *The Ed Sullivan Show, The Tonight Show, The Garry Moore Show, The Judy Garland*

Show, and *The Jack Paar Show.* In addition, she had been the recipient of the 1963 *Cue* magazine "Entertainer of the Year" Award, and she had also won The National Association of Record Merchandisers' "Best Selling Female Vocalist" award for that same year.

The same season, another well-known young recording artist and "TV singer," Steve Lawrence, made his Broadway debut as the star of the musical *What Makes Sammy Run?* Replacing Mr. Lawrence was another Broadway first-timer, pop singer Paul Anka. The very next Broadway season, RCA recording artist Sergio Franchi made his Broadway debut starring in the Richard Rodgers-Stephen Sondheim musical *Do I Hear A Waltz?*

It's interesting to note that all of the singers you've mentioned have appeared on Broadway as *replacements* in productions already running. It's common for producers to bring in a "name" at some point in a show's run (if they don't already have one) to give the box-office receipts a boost or, at least, in hopes that revenues won't drop, but that's certainly not new either. Let's take another look at *Funny Girl.* For those of you too young to remember—and for those who weren't born yet—it probably won't come as any surprise to learn that when Ms. Streisand's contract for *Funny Girl* was up, the big question was *who can possibly replace her?* According to the show's composer, Jule Styne, only one woman could fill the bill—the very popular comedienne and brilliant singer Mimi Hines. Ms. Hines, in her Broadway debut, took over the role to glowing reviews and managed, through her own star power, to keep *Funny Girl* running to packed houses for over a year and a half after Streisand's departure.

But how did the public *already* know Mimi Hines? Like so many others, through her many appearances on the national variety and talk shows of the day. So here was another case of an *already* famous entertainer debuting on Broadway. (More recently, Ms. Hines has returned to Broadway in the hit revival of *Grease!*)

Right across the street from *Funny Girl,* the musical *Hello, Dolly!* was also running, and a parade of "already famous" actresses filed in to replace its original star, Carol Channing. Among them was Phyllis Diller, one of the most popular television comics of that time, making *her* Broadway debut. These entertainers would go on to appear with even greater frequency than before on the talk and variety show circuit that emanated from New York. And, once again, media, music, comedy, and Broadway all fed each other on a national level. The big issue here—not new, but more pressing today due to ever-widening entertainment industry competition and rising theatrical production costs—is the need to capture the interest of the public at ever-escalating ticket prices.

So, then, there really is nothing new about a performer who is *already* famous making his or her Broadway debut?

Right. Besides those already mentioned, we can go back ten, twenty, thirty, forty years and more to see that this has almost always been the case. Angela Lansbury, for example, had *already* garnered two Academy Award nominations when she made her Broadway debut in the 1957 Broadway production *Hotel Paradiso.* Art Carney was *already* three times an Emmy Award winner for his portrayal of Ed Norton on *The Honeymooners* when he made his first Broadway appearance in 1957 in *The Rope Dancers.* Lucille Ball, at the height of her success on *I Love Lucy,* decided to tackle Broadway in the 1960 musical *Wildcat!* The sixties also brought to Broadway for the first time such name performers as Alan King (*The Impossible Years*), Anna Maria Alberghetti (*Carnival*), Albert Finney (*Luther*), and Melina Mercouri (*Illya, Darling!*). Also making their Broadway debuts in that same decade were the already famous Leslie Uggams (*Hallelujah, Baby!*), Eydie Gorme (*Golden Rainbow*), Joan Rivers (*Fun City*), and Mary Tyler

Moore and Richard Chamberlain (together in *Breakfast at Tif-fany's*). The seventies and eighties brought to Broadway for the first time such stars as Marlo Thomas (*Thieves*), Mark Hamill (*The Elephant Man*), Debbie Reynolds (*Irene*), Elizabeth Taylor (*The Little Foxes*), Raquel Welch (*Woman of the Year*), Cher (*Come Back to the Five and Dime, Jimmy Dean, Jimmy Dean*), Matt Dillon (*The Boys of Winter*), and, off Broadway, Farrah Fawcett (*Extremities*).

I'm not saying that these performers had no background on the stage—most of them did. I'm simply pointing out that they didn't appear on or off Broadway until *after* they had become famous. More recently we've seen Jessica Lange and Michelle Pfeiffer come to Broadway and off Broadway respectively with major film careers already under their belts. As I've said, however, when a name actor comes to Broadway or off Broadway, in *most* cases, that's where he or she started.

What about the occasional athlete-turned-actor who comes to Broadway or off Broadway—Cathy Rigby (*Peter Pan*), Greg Louganis (*Jeffrey* and *The Only Worse Thing You Could Have Told Me*), etc.? Surely *this* is new!

Afraid not. Who out there remembers the 1969 Broadway debut of world heavyweight champion Muhammed Ali in Oscar Brown Jr.'s *Buck White?* And this was a *musical!*

A word about Ms. Rigby and Mr. Louganis. Both trained rigorously as stage performers and did numerous productions in regional theater and summer stock (he in productions including *The Elephant Man, Equus,* and *Betrayal;* and she in *They're Playing Our Song, Paint Your Wagon,* and *The Wizard of Oz*) before trying out the New York scene.

It seems that the "star" names who work in the the-ater are more likely to come from television than from film. Why?

For one thing, a film career and a television career are different by nature. That is, an actor who is a regular on a hit series will be seen each week by millions and, for all intents and purposes, will be labeled a "television star" or, at least, a "television name." Also, when this series goes into syndication, the actor will stay in front of the public—sometimes for decades—and thus will maintain visibility to a good degree. Film careers usually take longer to build, and an actor's status as a "film star" can fluctuate widely and quickly depending on his or her track record at the box office. All of which means this: There are more actors who can be called "television stars" than there are actors who can be called "movie stars." In either case, very few *currently* popular television or film stars can make a long-term commitment to a play. Their film or television schedules usually preclude their doing so, and, of course, for most of them, doing theater is simply not a goal at this point in their careers. Therefore, when we see a star on or off Broadway, one of two elements is *usually* at work. The star is either committed to a very short run or else is trying to boost a sliding career with the exposure and media attention that doing a play in New York will offer. Almost never does an in-demand star commit to anything but the briefest of engagements in the New York theater. For example, at this writing there are several film stars on Broadway who are there essentially because they *need* to be there. The exception is Glenn Close, who is there because she *wants* to be there.

Which actors have recently crossed over from stage to screen?

Here is what is happening at this writing. Billy Crudup, who recently made his Broadway debut in Tom Stoppard's play *Arcadia*, within months was cast in a lead role opposite Robert DeNiro and Brad Pitt in the Barry Levinson film *Sleepers*, as well as in a major role in Woody Allen's latest feature. Donna

Murphy, shortly after winning a Tony for her performance in Stephen Sondheim's *Passion,* landed a featured role in the film *Jade,* starring David Caruso. Vicki Lewis, of the *Damn Yankees* revival, has since become a regular on the series *News-Radio.* Jude Law, within a few months of his acclaimed performance in the play *Indiscretions,* was tapped to co-star with Claire Danes in the feature film *I Love You, I Love You Not.* Jane Adams, fresh from her Tony-winning performance in Broadway's *The Inspector Calls,* was cast in a major role in Steve Martin's latest film, and the twice "Tony-ed" Stephen Spinella of *Angels in America* has since co-starred opposite Denzel Washington (another fine former stage actor) in *Virtuosity.* Michael Hayden, of Lincoln Center's recent revival of *Carousel,* has been cast as a regular on the Stephen Bochco series *Murder One;* Malcolm Gets, of Broadway's *The Moliere Comedies,* is now a cast member of NBC's *Caroline In the City;* and Marc Kudisch, of *Beauty and the Beast,* landed the title role in the ABC all-star television movie *Bye, Bye, Birdie.* Also, Melissa Errico, Eliza Doolittle of Broadway's recent revival of *My Fair Lady* starring Richard Chamberlain, became a series regular on *Central Park West,* as did Tom Verica, who was featured in *Prelude to a Kiss* on Broadway a few seasons back—the same play that launched the film career of Mary Louise Parker.

A handful of other "stage to screeners" from the past several years include Angela Bassett, Samuel L. Jackson, David Hyde Pierce, Gary Sinise, Jeanne Tripplehorn, Courtney B. Vance, Julianne Moore, Julianna Margulies, Steve Buscemi, John Leguizamo, Terry Kinney, David Strathairn, Christine Baranski, Dylan McDermott, Christine Lahti, Josh Hamilton, Roma Downey, James McDaniel, Nathan Lane, Steven Weber, Faith Prince, and by the time you read these words, a number of others, as well. Generally speaking, the higher the level of visibility and the greater the attention drawn to the actor (as the proliferation of Tony winners and nominees would seem to indicate), the greater the potential for crossover. Pervasive though it may be, the notion that actors "used to go from stage to screen, but nowadays it's the other way around" is not only negative and destructive, but—as the facts unfailingly continue to bear out season after season—it's also just plain wrong.

What are the benefits of working in student films and small independent films—as opposed to the stage—as a way of getting into more mainstream film ventures?

Largely, the benefits will be on-camera training, the experience of working with a film director (who may or may not move on to another level), and, hopefully, footage for your demo reel to show to agents and casting directors (the latter being more critical to the Los Angeles actor than to the New York actor). I say "hopefully" because the difficulty of tracking down directors and trying to get a copy of the film the actor was promised in exchange for appearing in it is an almost daily complaint that actors voice. Also, only a small percentage of independent films of this kind get major visibility, and compared to a successful play, most low-budget independent films remain relatively obscure.

There are, of course, exceptions! So *try to do both,* as many actors do. It should be of interest to note that many actors go straight from a major role in a high-profile stage production to a major film role or television series—and succeed at it brilliantly—without prior film experience. This begins to shoot down the common belief that, in terms of *craft,* the transition from "stage" acting to "screen" acting is a radical adjustment, no? There *are* differences between the two, but almost all of them get learned *after* the actor gets the job. Or, as a major television producer told a nervous young stage actor whom he'd just cast as a lead in a series, "*You* take care of the character; *we'll* take care of the cameras!"

Part Five:
Some Parting Pointers

I prefer my nonsmiling "legit" photograph to my commercial photo, although others who've seen both are divided in opinion. I always try to match the photo I'm sending to the nature of what's being cast (dramatic role, comedic role, etc.). There are times, however, when I'm not sure which photo is appropriate. Therefore, I end up sending both, which gets expensive. My smiling shot is the warmer and friendlier of the two, but the "legit" shot is prettier than the commercial shot—yet everyone says it looks *exactly* like me. Is there a solution so that I don't end up sending two photos and resumes?

Yes, there is. First, it's extremely common for actors to prefer their more dramatic shot, and at times it is indeed the better image of them. Generally speaking, though, your smiling photograph makes the better choice for the *photo postcard;* since the postcard is used for all-purpose follow-up, it should project your warmest and most engaging image. Assuming that you've chosen your smiling photo for your postcard, here is a suggestion. When you're leaning in the direction of sending your "legit" shot but you're indecisive as to which photo is appropriate, simply paperclip your smiling postcard to the resume side of your "legit" photo (taking care not to cover your most important credits, of course). This way, you've sent both images of yourself without sending two eight-by-tens with two resumes. Besides, you probably prefer your smiling postcard to your smiling eight-by-ten because the entire image has been minimized—just the way a movie we're not all that crazy about seems better on video than it does in the theater.

With respect to the "special skills" category on the resume, which skills carry the most weight?

Performance-related skills garner the greatest interest. These skills run the gamut from theatrically-oriented skills (mime, fencing, stage combat, rapier, etc.) to musical instrument skills to "circus-type" skills (juggling, unicycling, etc.) to strong athletic and trendy athletic skills (rollerblading) to foreign language skills (spoken with fluency).

A word about the latter. If you are fluent in a language or languages other than English, list this in first position in the special skills category on your resume (see Appendix A). Next, mark the language(s) with a highlighter and send your photo and resume along with a cover letter mentioning your language skills to all the voice-over agents listed in *Ross Reports Television* (see Appendix D). Highlight this information in your cover letter, too! Voice-over agents keep freelance lists of actors who have foreign language skills. Oftentimes, the more uncommon the language, the more likely you are to make the list. In any event, postcard these agents once a month reminding them of your language skills. In general, voice-over work is a very tough area of the industry to crack, yet the foreign language market is a niche that can provide some real income for those actors who qualify for it.

Casting directors, as well as agents, are featured guests at the "paid" seminars and workshops you discussed earlier. Can I assume that the results with casting directors will be the same as with agents? That is, do actors generally derive more benefit from meeting commercial casting directors than they will from meeting theatrical casting directors?

Interestingly, it's often just the opposite—due to the very different nature of the two areas themselves. Let me explain. Television commercial casting directors in New York (although not in Los Angeles) put their breakdowns out *directly to agents by telephone.* I'm not saying that they never refer actors to agents or give thought to actors they have met and call them in directly—they sometimes do. On the whole, however, it's easier for them to pick up the phone, call some really good commercial agents, and get what they need. In Los Angeles, also, where commercial auditions require a photo prescreen, commercial casting directors aren't likely to spend time looking for actors who have not been submitted by an agent.

Remember, however, that theatrical projects—on both coasts—usually require a submission of photos and resumes prior to an actor being granted an audition. Therefore, a *theatrical* casting director who is really impressed with an actor's work at a seminar—and who has a clear overview of the specifics of upcoming projects that will need casting—may then place the actor's photograph on file for a specific project in the future. Also, the actor can learn of theatrical projects and later submit a photo directly to the casting director. If that's what the casting director might be looking for, then the actor has a shot at getting an audition.

For all practical purposes, however, you usually will need an agent to get auditions with the necessary frequency required to "book" television commercials. So the irony is that while commercial representation is often easier to get than theatrical representation, commercial auditions are usually less accessible to the commercially unrepresented actor than theatrical auditions are to the theatrically unrepresented actor—at least for projects such as "legitimate" stage productions.

Another area in the theatrical division where I have seen actors obtain results is at seminars conducted by an assistant or associate soap opera casting director. This is because these assistants hire actors on a daily basis for extras and "under-fives" (see *AAB*, p. 29). For the actor who is considering meeting a soap opera assistant casting director in this fashion, let me offer a suggestion. There is a somewhat arcane "regulation" imposed by the top brass at soaps that supposedly requires soap opera casting personnel to put a six-month hold on hiring any actor they meet at a "paid" seminar. I say "arcane" because some soap casting personnel abide by it, others don't, and still others say they've never heard of any such regulation. There is an equally arcane loophole of sorts for the casting director—and therefore the actor—that says that this regulation does not apply to any actor who is *already* on file at the casting office. As I mentioned, some casting directors at soaps pay attention to this "rule," but most don't. Bottom line? Make sure that your photo and resume are on file with them and that you've followed up with at least a half-dozen—preferably more—photo postcards reporting your career progress *prior* to meeting with them at a seminar (see *AAB*, pp. 34–37). This will provide an advance "publicity campaign" of sorts before you meet them, and it will increase your chances of being hired.

Actors also can derive benefit at seminars with casting directors when the discussion turns to the specific kinds of audition material individual casting directors say they like to see and hear, as well as what they say they *don't* like to see and hear. For example, some casting directors clearly prefer not to hear monologues from plays by certain playwrights or songs from certain shows. And while most casting directors prefer monologues that have "active" conflict and deal with the immediate needs of a character, a few—but not too many—actually enjoy "story" monologues. Also, many casting directors want to see "you" in the part, while others want to see your ability to create characterization. Some casting directors don't like to see a piece that requires an accent, and others don't mind at all. There are also pieces that some casting directors say they don't ever want to see—or hear—again; others say they don't care how often they've seen or heard it as long as the actor does something fresh with it. Some casting directors even say that the most revealing information they get from an actor's monologue audition is the actual choice of the monologue itself! You get the picture, I'm sure: Audition material and how it's received is a highly subjective matter. Hopefully, how any piece is *performed* (also subjective) is what counts the most, but it certainly helps to know what kind of material individual casting directors enjoy and want to hear—as well as what they hate and wish they weren't listening to. After all, *you will be auditioning for them again in the future.*

Whether you meet casting directors in this fashion or not, the same suggestion applies here as with "paid" agent seminars. If you are not "audition ready," don't go, and if you are ready and you do go, do yourself a great service and also put your energies into auditioning under the most viable and traditional auspices possible.

As an actor who has been working more and more, I sometimes now get offers for two productions that conflict in schedule. Sometimes the choice to make is pretty obvious, but other times it presents a dilemma. Any guidelines for when I'm in a quandry?

Yes. The next time this happens, get a sheet of paper and draw a line straight down the center. On the left hand side, list in the following order: the title of the play, the role, the theater, the director, and the salary for offer number one. In the right hand column, do the exact same thing for offer number two. Now go down *both* columns and place a check mark next to your preference in each individual category. When you have finished, you will see that you have placed five check marks. One column will *always* have more check marks than the other. *Now* make your decision.

Besides tracking casting directors through publications such as *Theatrical Index, Regional Theatre Directory,* and *The Hollywood Reporter* (*AAB,* pp. 71– 86 and Appendix D of this book), are there any other direct approaches you can recommend for self-submission on a project?

Yes. Many actors have gotten excellent results by sending their materials (photo, resume, and cover letter) to the *director* of a specific project in addition to sending them to the casting director. A big part of the job of casting directors is to screen *out*—as well as screen *in*—actors for a given job. Directors, who typically get less mail than casting directors, will often grant an audition to an actor who has contacted them directly. In such instances, the director places the actor's name on his or her "list" and asks the casting director to set up an audition for the actor in question. I've seen the best results happen with this approach for theater projects, but I've also known it to work for film as well. And in one recent case, an actor I know landed a lead role in a television movie by making a videotape of the audition scene—which she had gotten through her agent, who had been unable to obtain an audition for her. This actor then sent the tape to the director in care of the network. The director figured what-the-hey, popped it into his VCR, and—duly impressed—showed it to the producer. The decision was made.

Theatrical Index and *The Hollywood Reporter* list the names of the *producers*—and, in the case of films, the production companies—of each project. In *Theatrical Index*, the producer's name is listed directly after the name of the play itself. In most cases, a photo and resume sent to a *director* of a specific project in care of the producer or production company will be passed on to the director.

Now, it will sometimes happen that the director of an upcoming project—for either Broadway or off Broadway—spends much of his or her time working in regional theater. To see if this is the case, consult the October "Season Preview" issue of *American Theatre* magazine. *American Theatre* lists by state each theater that is a constituent member theater of Theater Communications Group, the organization that publishes the magazine. Included, too, are all scheduled productions for the upcoming season at each theater, along with the name of the director for each production. For example, you might see a project you are right for in *Theatrical Index* that is scheduled to be produced on or off Broadway several months down the line. Then by cross-referencing with *American Theatre* you might also learn that this production's director will be involved with a project at a regional theater *prior* to the production for which you wish to audition. You could then send your materials to the director at this specific theater. If you write during the director's rehearsal period at this regional theater, you can be reasonably confident that he or she will receive your materials. In such a case, you will have covered yourself by writing to the director in care of the producer's office *and* at the regional theater as well.

Obviously, you also will have sent your materials to the *casting director* of the play. If you feel *very* passionately about the project, you can *also* send your photo, resume, and cover letter directly to the *playwright* in care of the playwright's agent, who will be listed in *Theatrical Index.*

An important note. *Be discriminating.* I don't recommend a blanket approach of mailing pictures and resumes to directors and/or playwrights. However, if you are aware of a *specific* project and you can express to the director (or playwright)— in writing—your *reason* for wanting to be seen, then by all means *go after it.* There will be times, of course, when you may not be certain if there is a role for you. Therefore, you may take a more general approach. That is, you can say in your letter, "If there is anything in your new production _____ for which you feel I may be suited, I would appreciate the opportunity to audition for you." Of course, you should also sincerely tell the director or playwright how you feel about his or her work. And while some might deny it to protect themselves from a deluge of mail, casting directors, directors, and playwrights are open to direct communication from an actor.

In doing the above, you will be functioning as your own agent. Daily I observe actors working effectively in this way. Agents, you see, are able to facilitate the casting process because they have *information* and *actors*. I recently made this point to an actor. He added, "But agents also have *clout*." The clout, I said, is a *result* of the *information* plus the *actor*. The agents' power is derivative of the clients they represent. Good clients equals clout. Bad clients equals no clout. With the youngest of actors being the exception, more and more agents are looking for actors to bring some semblance of a career to *them*. Therefore, whenever you can, go for the *work*.

All this gives me plenty to do to keep me busy for a while. Any final comments before you close?

To summarize, I think that the *business* aspect of the acting profession is largely about (1) letting people know who you are (photo, resume, cover letter); (2) telling them why they should want to see you by arousing interest and building credibility with progress reports in the form of postcards, flyers, notes, reviews, etc.; (3) finding out—in advance—specifically what they are doing by researching the publications and periodicals we've spoken about; so that (4) you can tell them why *they* need *you*. That is, telling those in a position to hire you—or represent you for others to hire—what they want to hear and need to know so that they will contact you.

Okay, now I'd like to ask *you* a question. Are you pleased that we have gotten through a lengthy discussion about communication, correspondence, effective follow-up, changing trends, creating career opportunities, and the like without ever once making use of that played-out, overworked, and odious 1980's term NETWORKING?? I know I am!

Appendix A:
Sample Resume
(New York Format)

Name
Unions

Service/Machine

Height: 5'11"
Weight: 165
Hair: Brown
Eyes: Blue

THEATER

OFF-BROADWAY	Hard Times	Ray Healey	Douglas Fairbanks Theater
	The Fantasticks	Matt	Sullivan Street Theater
STOCK	Album	Billy	Cumberland Lane Stage (Cumberland, R.I.)
	Mass Appeal	Mark	Foursquare Arts Center (Brighton, Mass.)
	Equus	Alan	C. T. Jones Theater (Lakeview, Maine)

| TELEVISION | All My Children | Tommy (recurring) | ABC |

COMMERCIALS   On-camera principals for national network and regional usage (tape upon request)

TRAINING   Acting: Two-year Meisner Technique program with Ron Stetson
Voice: Sara Krieger
Speech: Jean Lloyd
On-camera Commercial Technique: Bob Thomas

SPECIAL SKILLS   Fluent German, saxophone, football, soccer, racquetball, golf, swimming, rock climbing, whitewater rafting

Appendix B: Sample Resume (Los Angeles Format)

Name
Unions

Service/Machine

Height: 5'7"
Weight: 125
Hair: Blonde
Eyes: Brown

FILM

| The Giant Within | Anne (featured) | Touchstone Pictures (Jan Reed, Director) |

TELEVISION

Murder One	Guest Star	ABC
The Client	Guest Star	CBS
Melrose Place	Guest Star	Fox

THEATER

Jenny Kissed Me	Jenny	Old London Rep Co.
Veronica's Room	Veronica	Boland Arts Festival
Vanities	Joanne	Southwick Stage Co.
Biloxi Blues	Daisy	West Civic Theatre

COMMERCIALS

On-camera principals for national network and overseas usage (tape upon request)

TRAINING

Acting: Jean Ann Edwards (Two Years)
Speech: Tom Carlin
Dance: Jim Powers (ballet), Laura Roberts (jazz)

SPECIAL SKILLS

Piano, clarinet, oboe, aerobics, diving, gymnastics, tennis

Appendix C: New York and Los Angeles Daytime Serials

NEW YORK

ABC-TV
All My Children
The City

CBS-TV
As The World Turns
Guiding Light

NBC-TV
Another World

LOS ANGELES

ABC-TV
General Hospital
One Life to Live

CBS-TV
The Bold and the Beautiful
The Young and the Restless

NBC-TV
Days of Our Lives

Appendix D: Periodicals and Publications

Academy Players Directory, published three times annually by the Academy of Motion Picture Arts and Sciences, 8949 Wilshire Blvd., Beverly Hills, California 90211.

American Theatre magazine, published ten times annually by Theatre Communications Group, 355 Lexington Avenue, New York, New York 10017.

Back Stage, published weekly by BPI Communications, Inc., 1515 Broadway, New York, New York 10036.

Drama-Logue, published weekly by Drama-Logue Inc., 1456 N. Gordon Street, Hollywood, California 90028.

The Hollywood Reporter, published daily (except Saturdays and Sundays) by H. R. Industries, Inc., 5055 Wilshire Blvd., Los Angeles, California 90036.

L.A. Weekly, published weekly by L.A. Weekly, Inc., P.O. Box 29905, Los Angeles, California 90029.

Players' Guide, published annually by Paul Ross, 165 W. 46th St., New York, New York 10036.

Regional Theatre Directory, published annually by Theatre Directories, P.O. Box 519, Dorset, Vermont 05251. (Tel.: (802) 867-2223).

Ross Reports Television, published monthly by Television Index, Inc., 40-29 27th St., Long Island City, New York 11101.

Ross Reports USA, published twice annually by Television Index, Inc., 40-29 27th St., Long Island City, New York 11101.

Soap Opera Weekly, published weekly by K-III Corporation, 41 W. 25th St., New York, New York 10010.

Theater Week, published weekly by That New Magazine, Inc., 28 W. 25th St., New York, New York 10010.

Theatrical Index, published weekly by Price Berkley, 888 8th Avenue, New York, New York 10019.

Appendix E: Recommended Reading

Callan, K. 1988. *The Los Angeles Agent Book*. Studio City, CA: Sweden Press.

———. 1989. *The New York Agent Book*. Studio City, CA: Sweden Press.

Cohen, Robert. 1990. *Acting Professionally: Raw Facts About Careers in Acting*. Mountain View, CA: Mayfield Publishing Co.

Donnelly, Kyle, ed. 1992. *Classical Monologues for Men*. Portsmouth, NH: Heinemann.

———. 1992. *Classical Monologues for Women*. Portsmouth, NH: Heinemann.

Eaker, Sherry, comp. and ed. 1995. *The Back Stage Handbook for Performing Artists*. New York: Back Stage Books.

Lewis, M. K., and Rosemary Lewis. 1989. *Your Film Acting Career*. Santa Monica, CA: Gorham House.

Litwak, Mark. 1986. *Reel Power*. New York: Plume.

O'Neil, Brian. 1993. *Acting As a Business*. Portsmouth, NH: Heinemann.

Searle, Judith. 1991. *Getting the Part*. New York: Simon & Schuster.

Shurtleff, Michael. 1980. *Audition*. New York: Bantam.

Steele, William. 1992. *Stay Home and Star!* Portsmouth, NH: Heinemann.

Wolper, Andrea. 1992. *The Actor's City Sourcebook*. New York: Back Stage Books.